Imperium Press was founded in 2018 to supply students and laymen with works in the history of rightist thought. If these works are available at all in modern editions, they are rarely ever available in editions that place them where they belong: outside the liberal weltanschauung. Imperium Press' mission is to provide right thinkers with authoritative editions of the works that make up their own canon. These editions include introductions and commentary which place these canonical works squarely within the context of tradition, reaction, and counter-Enlightenment thought—the only context in which they can be properly understood.

NEMESIS

THE JOUVENELIAN VS.
THE LIBERAL
MODEL OF HUMAN ORDERS

C.A. BOND

PERTH
IMPERIUM PRESS
2019

Published by Imperium Press

www.imperiumpress.org

FIRST EDITION

A catalogue record for this
book is available from the
National Library of Australia

ISBN 978-0-6486905-1-1 Paperback
ISBN 978-0-6486905-2-8 e-book

CONTENTS

PREFACE

THIS book developed from my dissatisfaction with the nature of political discourse and recent political developments. This led me to ask very basic questions as to why changes occurred when they did, how these changes came about as they did, and why they happened at all—I soon came to appreciate that modern political thought cannot answer any of these questions. In the course of this questioning I happened to be directed to a blog which seemed to provide the answers I sought, this being the Unqualified Reservations blog written by Mencius Moldbug. Any reader who has also read this blog will recognize that this book owes an enormous debt to it. The reader may justifiably ask why it is, then, that instead of writing a commentary on Moldbug's thought, I wrote one on Bertrand de Jouvenel's work *On Power*. The answer is that I believed, and still do, that Moldbug's most valuable thought was derived from Jouvenel's theoretical model of power. It is this aspect that I wished to develop and in considering this aspect to be particularly valuable it required that a great deal of Moldbug's further thought, and many concepts, had to be rejected as incompatible with this specific model. To outline which elements of his thought I believed should be amended or rejected would be exceptionally complicated, and far less fruitful than merely accepting the invaluable contribution he has made in rediscovering and developing Jouvenel's thought, and then pursuing the incomplete avenues of thought to which it points. As a result, the book begins with Jouvenel and not Moldbug, and any theory contained in the book which subsequently runs parallel to that developed by Moldbug is fully acknowledged here as reliant on his work.

Having concluded that those aspects of Moldbug's writing which convincingly explained modern political developments were underpinned by Jouvenel's theoretical framework, I found that I had to engage with Jouvenel's work in much the same way as I had done with Moldbug's—that is, I had to take Jouvenel's core theoretical claims and engage in a process of critiquing those other elements of his thought which appear to be incompatible with it. At this juncture I was fortunate enough to discover the work of Alasdair MacIntyre, whose work in the realm of traditions has convinced me of the necessity of rationality being embodied in traditions. This framework provided me with a sophisticated elaboration of what I had been doing quite naturally. That is, it allowed me to clearly and precisely recognize that various traditions of thought were present in both *On Power* and Moldbug's blog which I believe I have been able to disentangle in this work—the two fundamental traditions being first, the modern individualistic tradition of modernity, and second, the very different tradition implied by Jouvenel's theoretical model of the centrality of human orders.

To maintain focus within this work, I have been less concerned with developing thought which follows from the framework of human centrality than I have with critiquing the modern individualistic tradition. To do this, I have attempted to demonstrate that the Jouvenelian theoretical model provides strong grounds for explaining the latter tradition's development. This book is, therefore, an attempt to first provide a theoretical basis for this alternative tradition of centrality, and to then demonstrate how this tradition better explains political developments than does the individualistic tradition of modernity and its various offshoots. For this reason I have attempted to explain the development of such phenomena as the individual, sovereignty, philosophical schools of thought, and modern political science, among others. It would have been possible to include countless other examples which likewise support the arguments made in this book, and I hope that further works will follow to give these areas the attention they deserve.

In writing this book, I have been especially indebted to those who have, over the years, engaged in prolonged and detailed discussion of the theoretical implications of Moldbug's and Jouvenel's work, two of whom I wish to draw special attention to despite never having met in person—these being @MrScientism and Adam Katz, who have offered invaluable constructive dialogue.

We are exceptionally fortunate to live in a time when instantaneous communication between people across great distances is possible, and when a great many works are instantly available anywhere in the world, something which allows entirely new schools of thought to congregate and flourish online, making such work as this possible—a work inspired by a blog, and developed through further blogs, email discussions, forums, and twitter exchanges with anonymous individuals and utilizing newly digitized resources. I have no illusions that such a work would have been impossible within the confines of academia, as some of the conclusions are literally unthinkable from the traditions institutionalized within our schools.

NEMESIS

I

THE MODEL INTRODUCED

THE purpose of this work is to present, and then further develop, a model of political understanding which in many ways radically differs from those which dominate our modern understanding of how human orders form. The model that will provide the theoretical basis of this work was created and introduced by the political theorist Bertrand de Jouvenel in *On Power: The Natural History of its Growth.*[1] As can be deciphered from the title, the focal point of Jouvenel's model is something which he termed "Power."[2] Writing the work as he did in the midst of WWII, Jouvenel was, like many of his contemporaries, occupied with the vast expansion of centralised governance throughout the world, something which had lent itself to the modern phenomenon of total war. Where Jouvenel differed from his contemporaries was in pursuing an avenue of political theory which explained this centralisation within a historical setting, and which connected the expansion of governance with a conception of human orders which was radically illiberal.

Key to Jouvenel's model is the assumption that there is a con-

1 Bertrand de Jouvenel, *On Power: Its Nature and the History of Its Growth* (New York: Viking Press, 1949).

2 As noted in the Translator's Note to *On Power*, "the word 'Power', whenever it begins with a capital letter, denotes the central governmental authority in states of communities."

3

stant structure of human orders; human orders are invariably and unavoidably centralised, and this centralised order itself breaks down into a pattern of three distinct categories. The first of these categories is a centre. This centre in Jouvenel's conception may be occupied by an institution or institutions, or, importantly, it may not be occupied by something corporeal. Regardless of whether this centre is occupied, all human orders are invariably focused around this shared centre of attention. As a result, this centre is the most important aspect of this model, as it is the relationship of all other categories to this centre, and subsequently to the other categories of this order, that infuses this model with regularity.

The second category is comprised of subsidiary centres of power which exist outside of this centre. These subsidiary centres can be seen as delegates of the centre, and act in its name and under its authority. Jouvenel termed the elements that comprise this category "social authorities,"[3] and by this he meant such entities as the nobility, families, corporations, trade unions, and any other institution within an order which can demand the obedience and allegiance of those within that order in conjunction with the central governing apparatus, or Power.

The final category is the periphery, which is that part of an order which exists outside of the subsidiary centres of power. It is governed by them, and in being governed by them, finds its relationship to the centre of society mediated by them.

Defining the institutions and actors that occupy these various categories according to some set criteria is not particularly fruitful. Humans repeatedly invent new forms of organisation, and ways of life vary from one order to another, and even over time, but this does not mean that we cannot identify who in a given order occupies what position. The means by which we can identify who is in what position, irrespective of whether we are considering a medieval monarchy or a 20th century democracy, is by giving primacy to the structural arrangement of our model, and then identifying which institutions and actors are acting in ways predicted by this constant structure. Our next step must then be to explain what the predicted behaviours of these various categories are, so that we can recognise them.

In Jouvenel's theory, the primary centre of power—or "Pow-

---

3 Jouvenel, *On Power*, 130.

er"—is envisioned as a development which has, through the course of history, become embodied in standing institutions. That Jouvenel considers this centrality to be a constant, regardless of whether it is occupied by an institution, is evident in numerous sections of *On Power*, particularly when he considers the origins of Power.[4] For Jouvenel, this centre, once it has become embodied by an institution, becomes at base a fundamentally selfish and predatory entity. However, where Jouvenel departs from what would appear to be a standard liberal position on the role of central government is that he also recognises that this account is incomplete, and that there is an inescapably social nature to this Power. The significance of this cannot be overstated, as in so doing, Jouvenel breaks, however imperfectly, from the accounts of modernity that consider this government to be nothing better than a "necessary evil."[5] The nature of this Power, possessing as it does this dual psychology, will then become in Jouvenel's words:

> …at once the symbol of the community, its mystical core, its cohesive force, its sustaining virtue. But it is also ambition for itself, the exploitation of society, the will to power, the use of the national resources for purposes of prestige and adventure.[6]

By recognising the complex and subtle nature of this central Power, instead of treating it with reflexive disdain, Jouvenel opened up the possibility of considering this aspect of his model with a clarity unavailable to those operating within a liberal tradition. Specifically, Jouvenel was able to see the means and mechanisms by which the centre makes appeals to the social good. While there are a number of issues with this conception of this central Power, for now it is a sufficient characterisation for our purposes of un-

---

4 Even in the supposedly egalitarian orders, Jouvenel notes that this centrality was occupied by the gods, something which has also been noted by the anthropologists David Graeber and Marshall Sahlins who make the point that these supposedly egalitarian orders are deeply embedded within a metaphysical hierarchy. See David Graeber and Marshall Sahlins, *On Kings* (Chicago: Hau Books, 2017).
5 Thomas Paine's opinion that "Society in every state is a blessing, but Government, even in its best state, is but a necessary evil; in its worst state an intolerable one" is emblematic of the standard liberal conception of the character of government. Thomas Paine, *Common Sense* (Philadelphia: Robert Bell, 1776).
6 Jouvenel, *On Power*, 84.

derstanding the basis of the model.

The result of being able to recognise this dual character of Power is that a key mechanism of Power's expansion becomes visible, this being the manner in which this central Power naturally makes appeals to the periphery of society as a means to engage in indirect and subversive conflict against its own subsidiaries. This process creates a great deal of confusion in modern political thought as this is counterintuitive. Within this thought, it is assumed that the subsidiaries of an order are in alliance with the central Power, given that they are all elements of the same governance structure ranged against, in modernity, the individual. This is false. While in a general sense the subsidiaries uphold the overall order, in reality these two categories are in a state of constant tension and conflict which merely varies in its intensity. The peripheral element, to which this central Power makes its appeal, is normally the largest element of the model, and represents the section of society identified as existing outside the sphere of the central Power and also outside the subsidiary centres of power. Be this the proletariat, the plebeians, the poor, the people, the masses, or whatever specific form this category takes within a given order. This periphery is always identified as being in some way oppressed and in need of some form of political empowerment by whichever actor is forming an alliance with it. The periphery often becomes a valuable asset to those with an interest in altering a given order due to the fact that it represents a pool of willing and loyal participants in the conflict between centres of power which can be used in efforts to undermine other centres of power. It is notable that the formal reasons cited for such an alliance between a power and a section of the periphery are invariably framed in terms of a breach of the ethical standards of the order in question, and that this breach is inevitably premised on the basis of equality in some sense.

At times, it is this Power which aligns with the periphery as a means to strengthen itself and weaken the subsidiary power centres; at other times, it is the subsidiary power centres which engage with the periphery to undermine and overtake the primary Power. Whatever section is aligning with this periphery, it should be noted that without this alliance between a power centre and the periphery, the periphery is itself basically irrelevant. Without

the assistance of a centre of power, any action by the p
by virtue of lacking institutional embodiment and poli.
tection, at best sporadic and ineffective. A popular prot.
bellion, or any other form of dissenting action by the perip
if it has no support from an element in the power structure, v.
quickly fade into irrelevance; if it does have this support, it will
find itself supplied with resources, exposure, protection, and institutional embodiment. This theoretical model, therefore, precludes
the possibility of successful rebellion and dissent without the con-
nivance of some element of a power structure (or an element of an
external power structure, as shall become clear in later chapters).
That such alliances could form between a centre of power and the
periphery is the result of these allies finding themselves with a
joint enemy in the shape of other centres of power. For example,
to the central Power, subsidiary powers are competitors who are
always seeking to limit and control the central Power. To the periphery, the subsidiaries are the immediate manifestations of irk-
some authority that burden it with what it sees as petty tyrannies.
They are, therefore, both in alignment against the subsidiaries for
different reasons, but in alignment nonetheless, and this is why, in
this conflict between the central Power and the subsidiaries, the
periphery generally aligns with the central Power. In doing so, the
periphery facilitates the central Power's replacement of the subsidiaries. Of course, this is not seen in this manner; instead, this
realignment of obedience to the central Power alone is presented by the central Power, quite naturally, as simply the liberation
of the periphery and not the replacement of one authority (the
subsidiaries) by another (itself). The periphery, likewise, sees this
process as one of liberation and not as the taking on of a new
authority, and it is in this hope, according to Jouvenel, that we
find the "main reason for the endless complicity of subjects in the
designs of Power; it is the true secret of Power's expansion."[7]

If the centre and the periphery act in this way according to
the model, then what of the subsidiary centres? The subsidiary's
nature is to be the resistance against the expansion of the central
Power; it is its "business,"[8] as Jouvenel writes of aristocracy:

7 Jouvenel, *On Power,* 130.
8 ibid., 188.

and everywhere, opposes the rise of a
es in its own right of sufficient means
lf independent of society, those means
ermanent administration, a standing

, just as with the central Power, seen
.. in nature. They seek to protect their own ex-
...u, if possible, to enlarge their power, but they also view
tnemselves in a social sense. Jouvenel describes the nature of these
subsidiaries, as well as criticises the inability of mainstream political theory to recognise their relationship to the central Power, in
the following passage:

> The mistake of not seeing in society more than the one
> Power, i.e. the governmental or public authority, has an as-
> tonishingly wide vogue. Whereas in fact the governmental
> is but one of the authorities present in society; there exists
> alongside it a whole host of others, which are at once its col-
> laborators, in that they help it in securing social order, and its
> rivals, in that, like it, they claim men's obedience and inveigle
> them into their service.[10]

The relationship of these subsidiary power centres to the primary
Power within an order is the pivotal relationship within our model. Do these subsidiary centres hold a strong position vis-à-vis the
central Power? Are they aligned and clearly under control? How
these two categories interact and their relative status is key, as we
shall see throughout this book.

Now that we have established the various categories and have
noted their general behaviours and dispositions, we can follow
Jouvenel in providing concrete examples which support the theoretical model. The primary example employed by Jouvenel was
that of European monarchies, which increased in power over the
course of the medieval and early modern period at the expense
not only of the lords and barons that governed in their name,
but also of the Church. Jouvenel shows quite clearly that this expansion was achieved by appealing to the rest of the structure

9   Jouvenel, *On Power*, 179.
10   ibid., 129.

that was governed by these subsidiary centres, and by directing popular sentiment against them: an appeal to the periphery. Unfortunately, in our attempts to briefly recount Jouvenel's history of monarchy, we will encounter a problem which Jouvenel himself recognised: that the modern reader's inherited knowledge of monarchy will undoubtedly be limited, if not grossly distorted, by misconceptions ingrained by modern political thought. This will be the case for almost everyone barring academic specialists in medieval history, so the reader should not take this as a reproach.

To remedy modern misunderstandings of monarchy, and to assist the reader in understanding the historical examples used by Jouvenel, requires that first, we dispute the popular conception of monarchy, and that second, we provide a more accurate account. The modern interpretation of monarchy that I am referring to is one which understands monarchy as a system of governance within which a king or a queen rules in a fairly arbitrary fashion in collusion with nobility and the Church. In the popular understanding of history (and in mainstream political thought), this form of government was replaced sometime around the 17th century in England, the 18th century in France, and later in all other nations, by revolutions of the people which ushered in modernity.[11] Democracy was supposedly implemented in their wake, and governance was then placed in the hands of the equal people. The implication at the base of this modern understanding is that governance has progressed from being centralised to being dispersed and decentralised in the form of the people's self-government, a process which has reached its conclusion with modern liberal democracy. This, as we shall see, is precisely backwards.

The historical origins of kingship are lost to time, and while there are many interesting speculations that can be made from the information available to us, it is not important for our purposes to do so. Instead, we can follow Jouvenel's lead and begin with the Germanic kingdoms that arose in the wake of the Roman Empire's collapse. These Germanic kingdoms—the Franks, Lombards, Ostrogoths, Visigoths, etc.—were administered such that between the monarchs and the commoners were many layers of authority. The common man would have been beholden to a

---

11 The archetypal form of this history is, of course, Whig history which underpins political discourse in the Western world.

noble who may himself have been beholden to another noble, and this is before we even consider the role of the Church and the obligations required by it. This was a world wherein exactly who had obligations to whom was not always clear. Further, the kings themselves had a very limited area of influence within which they held full control. Outside of the monarch's own immediate sphere (the court), he relied on the acquiescence of a sometimes intransigent nobility. We can see this relative weakness of the early kings when we look at the nature of kingship under Phillip Augustus, who reigned as the King of France between 1180 and 1223. As Jouvenel takes pains to point out, Phillip Augustus had no regular system of taxation, no standing army of any kind, no governmental officials, and little wealth beyond his own estates. This was a comparable state of affairs to other contemporary monarchs in Europe. Now, compare this to Louis XIV who reigned as the King of France between 1638 and 1715. Louis XIV had a widespread permanent taxation system, a standing army of around 200,000 men, a police force answerable to his court, and a specialised governmental apparatus.[12] Clearly, the reader can appreciate from this that a serious increase in centralisation must have occurred in the intervening years.

To achieve this obvious centralisation, the kings from Phillip onwards in France, and likewise the competing kings and queens throughout Europe, engaged in chronic conflict, not with the commoners, but with the nobility and the Church. Granted, on a day-to-day basis all three institutions would have combined to uphold the given order, and so would have, for all intents and purposes, presented a united front against the commoners, yet this merely distracts from the fact that over the centuries, and in complex ways, this constellation of authorities engaged in chronic internecine conflict. The nature of this conflict is revealed when we consider the techniques employed by the monarchy to circumvent its need to govern in conjunction with the nobility and the Church.

The ability of these monarchies to centralise control ebbed and flowed with the availability of tools at the monarch's disposal. Such tools included taxation, coinage, military reform, and law. We can begin by considering the ways in which coinage and tax-

12 Jouvenel, *On Power*, 127–28.

ation developed.

With the arrival of the Germanic kingdoms, we find that the Roman taxation system and the circulation of coinage inherited by these kingdoms seem to have all but disappeared. These non-monetary kingdoms operated on a system of land dispersal, where land was granted to vassals from whom they could provision their own forces. It appears that a similar process occurred in the Near East, where land reforms were instigated as a means to maintain an army following the collapse of the Byzantine coinage system.[13] In the West, such an arrangement required a substantial devolution of power to the local lords, who were granted the land to maintain. The monarchs had to rely on the lords agreeing to supply men and resources under the lords' immediate control, which presents a case of subsidiary power centres having a great deal of leverage vis-à-vis the primary Power centre.

The first stirrings of the centralisation of monarchy become apparent with attempts by monarchs to reintroduce coinage on a large scale.[14] This may seem somewhat surprising given the modern economic assumption that money is both natural and an extension of barter, but this is erroneous. To understand why monarchs would wish to implement a coinage system, we need to understand that a monetary system is not a natural and spontaneous affair, but, rather, one that requires an organised supply of metal and coin in the form of mining and minting, and an organised market in which the coin is to be traded. Money also requires a demand which is itself not spontaneous. All of these aspects of a monetary system have to be created with great effort, but despite

13   For an account of Byzantine reforms in the wake of this collapse which led to recompense in the form of land, see Peter Spufford, *Money and Its Use in Medieval Europe* (Cambridge: Cambridge University Press, 1988), 15–16.

14   Spufford also makes the interesting claim that this reintroduction (or simply the introduction) of coinage was often on the advice of newly arrived Christian advisers in the courts of Christianised monarchs: "The most reasonable hypothesis linking coinage and Christianity seems to be that, along with the official acceptance of Christianity, the rulers of these countries took leading missionaries into the circle of their intimate advisers, and that these men, coming out from societies in which coinage was an accepted and expected attribute of sovereignty, advised their new patrons that they too ought to strike coin. These new coinages also come at a point in time when kingship was being exalted, and contributed to it. Official Christianity and an official coinage both came soon after the first steps towards the making of a monarchical state out of hitherto tribal societies." Spufford, *Money and its Use in Medieval Europe*, 83.

this effort the benefits are great for a centralising power.[15]

We must consider that a coinage system bestows on the minting authority a source of profit in the form of reminting and debasement, a form of monetary manipulation which also weakens subsidiaries by making their wealth depreciate in comparison to those who are minting coins. This coinage system also allows the central Power to engage in disintermediated relationships with elements it would previously have been unable to engage. Money, for example, allows the purchase of mercenaries who can be used in lieu of the nobility, thereby offering the central Power access to a body of men directly loyal to itself. In addition, once this system is widespread, the possibility of transferring wealth over long distances becomes feasible. Discharging feudal dues in the form of produce is an inherently localised system; discharging it in coinage is not. This implementation of a widespread coinage and a taxation system premised on coin then makes it possible for the king's court to reside in one place indefinitely, and so we see the development of capital cities following the establishment of coinage systems.

This transfer of wealth in the form of taxation premised on coinage did not revive in a sustained way until the 13th century, and this resulted from the successful integration of feudal territories into centralised kingdoms. It is at this point that we see the mass expansion of money relationships brought about by the demand for money created by landlords and monarchs in allowing contracts to be discharged in the form of money as opposed to services.[16] Again, this did not occur spontaneously, and was driven by the centralising power centres. This increased liquidity of wealth in the form of currency also opened the door to papal taxation systems, with the Papacy implementing taxation of churches for the funding of the Fourth and Fifth Crusades, a development which was maintained continually thereafter, and provided the resources necessary for the continual centralising actions of the

---

15   For a full account of the manner in which markets and monetary systems have been the creation of authority, see David Graeber, *Debt: The First 5,000 Years* (New York: Melville House, 2011).

16   For an account of the development of monetary demand in the 13th century, see Peter Spufford, "The Place of Money in the Commercial Revolution of the Thirteenth Century," in *Money and its Use in Medieval Europe*, 240–66.

Papacy itself.[17] In all other territories, taxation was likewise introduced under the pretence of necessity due to war, and it was eventually retained as an ongoing process even in times of peace. As Jouvenel notes, this development opened the door not only to the occasional payment of mercenaries, but ultimately to the creation and maintenance of standing armies.[18]

The creation of standing armies provides the next prong of centralisation, since a major problem encountered by central Powers was their inability to maintain effective and reliable fighting forces. Their vassals were not professional soldiers, and the monarchs were greatly hampered by the ability of the nobles to simply refuse service, or to only supply men and resources for fixed periods in accordance with feudal arrangements. The initial solution to this problem was to hire mercenaries for money, and then to provide for markets where this money could be used. To encourage the supply of goods to this market, there had to be a demand for coin which was brought about by having a monetary taxation system not acceptable in the form of in-kind services, as with the English Geld system. Such a development creates a relatively closed circulation, and forces a market system into place.[19] In line with this development was the possibility of forming large scale armies of infantry troops that could defeat cavalry, as Jouvenel notes:

> Infantry did not become capable of withstanding cavalry charges until the Swiss had revived the Greek tactical formation of the "hedgehog": and it was only then that, backed by plebeian mercenaries, the monarchy could make itself absolute.[20]

Jouvenel explains the reasoning behind this development by the vivid example of the Janissaries of the Ottoman Empire,[21] a force

---

17 Spufford, *Money and its Use in Medieval Europe*, 157.

18 Jouvenel, *On Power*, 142.

19 For an account of mercenary market supply and of the logistical difficulties of creating such markets leading to their replacement by organised logistics, see Volker Bach, "Markets for Mercenaries: Supplying Armies in Sixteenth-Century Germany," in *Food & Markets: Proceedings of the Oxford Symposium on Food and Cookery 2014*, ed. Mark Williams (London: Prospect Books, 2015) 35–43.

20 Jouvenel, *On Power*, 182.

21 ibid., 183.

comprised of Christian slaves from the Balkans who were the core of the Sultan's fighting force—not, as would be expected, the Islamic nobility. This pattern of the periphery being conscripted into forces directly answerable to the central Power is repeated throughout history. We could add many more examples, such as the Swiss Guards of the French Court, Ivan the Terrible's Oprichnik, or the Varangian Guard of the Byzantine Emperors. The monarchies, now able to provision their own forces that were loyal directly to them, and also reliant on them alone, could now act without the hindrance of the nobility.

Another area where the actions of the centralising monarchs can be seen undermining subsidiary centres of power is in the increasing centralisation of law, and on this point the examples of the legal reforms of Henry II are instructive. It is important, first, to note that the nature of law in pre-modern societies was very different from that of its present incarnation. Law was very much dispersed and decentralised; moreover, it was verbal and unwritten, with many local courts that did not answer directly to the central Power of their given order. Also, this central Power was not seen as the source of law, something we don't observe until the development of the concept of sovereignty, with its assertion of the sovereign origin of law in the 16th century. Henry II's reforms are clearly marked by an intrusion on these local centres of law, with not only local barons' courts being undermined, but also ecclesiastical courts. This attempt to submit ecclesiastical law to the authority of monarchical law led to the famous murder of Thomas Becket, the Archbishop of Canterbury, who objected to this development.[22] It is also notable that these reforms were specifically marked by an expanded availability of legal writs to the medieval class of freemen who were not under the jurisdiction of the barons' courts.[23] The reader should bear in mind that to be a freeman in medieval England required that the person was under no feudal obligation to a local lord and was under the authori-

22 For a comprehensive review of the nature of this conflict between Thomas Becket and Henry II over the issue of legal jurisdiction, see Michael Staunton, *Thomas Becket and His Biographers* (Woodbridge: The Boydell Press, 2006).
23 Richard Hudson, "The Judicial Reforms of the Reign of Henry II," *Michigan Law Review*, Vol. 9, No. 5 (March 1911): 385–95. http://www.jstor.org/stable/1275164.

ty of the king alone. Here we have a clear example of the king empowering a section of society at the expense of the subsidiary centres of power, and the act being labelled a grant of freedom. To be free in this conception, therefore, meant to be free of *local* obligations only, and not of obligations to *the king*, and so not free *simpliciter*.[24]

These attempts by the monarchs to centralise using these various means could not have succeeded without assistance. The monarch needed institutions and bodies of men to staff these institutions. The source of this manpower was (normally) neither the nobility nor the higher members of the ecclesiastic order, but the commoners whom, in popular understanding, the monarchs were supposedly oppressing. It was members of this peripheral section of the medieval order that passed "its uneventful life outside the proud pyramids of aristocracy"[25] who were invited into the king's court, who staffed his legal system, who entered into governmental service, and who peopled his armies. Where monarchs could not call on these commoners, they could also call in foreign elements, be they Italian or Jewish bankers, or foreign mercenaries. The alliance between the commoners or foreign elements and the monarchy then comes to the fore, and here we can see the true nature of this centralisation. The monarchs (the central Powers) entered into an alliance with the periphery (commoners, as well as foreign elements) so as to distance themselves from the subsidiary centres of power (the nobility and the Church).

So as the reader can now see, there are ample historical examples to which Jouvenel's theoretical model can be applied, and the level of insight it supplies into these examples is unmatched by competing political theories. This does not mean that the theoretical model is by any means perfect, as there are many aspects of Jouvenel's work which present serious issues from an angle of theoretical coherency. The source of these issues are, I believe,

---

24 The idea of being free simpliciter, in the common understanding of the word, is here shown to be deeply incorrect, but it has remarkable implications for our current state of affairs, because this is precisely the role the free people of a democracy hold in relation to the state. This is a point which forms a central part of Jouvenel's work, as he takes pains to distinguish a liberty created by one's own ability to enforce it from a liberty granted to one by a greater power, as we shall see in chapter 2.

25 Jouvenel, *On Power*, 85.

rooted in Jouvenel's failure to apply this model consistently to the evidence at hand, and instead to revert to assumptions which were entirely unwarranted by the theoretical framework he presented—the sources of these assumptions being themselves rooted in the underlying liberal beliefs which he held. We can now turn our attention to understanding how these liberal beliefs impinged upon Jouvenel's work, and we can consider whether there is justification for maintaining these assumptions, or alternatively, whether the model should take priority, and these assumptions should be discarded.

II

THE INDIVIDUALISTIC MODEL VS. THE JOUVENELIAN MODEL

In chapter 1, we presented something that we identified as the Jouvenelian model, within which human orders are divided into three interacting segments: a primary Power, subsidiary power centres, and a periphery. This interpretation of Jouvenel's work opens us up to the justifiable accusation of misrepresentation because this is a rather selective presentation of *On Power*. Jouvenel does not simply model society in this fashion, but instead presents a more complicated picture of developments. This additional complication is, however, not to Jouvenel's credit, but instead results from a conflation of two distinct and contradictory underlying models of human organisation. The first of the two models was presented to the reader in chapter 1; we can label this model the Jouvenelian model. Within this model, all that occurs within a given order is invariably constrained, and ultimately determined, by the centres of power which comprise that order's constellation of authorities. There is no apparent potential for anything like a spontaneous order emerging from the ground up through individual action. The second model maintained by Jouvenel is a model of human orders premised on them being comprised of discrete individuals, a model which will be familiar to the reader as the basis of modernity. It is this second model which enables Jouvenel to view aspects of this order as spontaneous, and as capable of developing irrespective of the centres of power that comprise the given order. It will be our contention that by systematically removing this second model from Jouvenel's work, or, at the very least, by curtailing it, we can drastically improve the clarity of the first model. Furthermore, it will be our contention that this first model can account for the development and dominance of the second model in the modern era. One of the more productive approaches to demonstrating the problems created by Jouvenel's maintenance of these two competing models of human orders is by beginning with his adherence to a liberty of the individual which, in many ways, forms the underlying motivation for why Jouvenel wrote the work he did.

For Jouvenel, there are, broadly speaking, two conceptions of liberty present in political thought. The first form of liberty is a liberty granted by a higher power; the second form of liberty is a liberty obtained by one's own strength.[1] According to Jouvenel, liberty of the first kind is inferior, and in essence, a false liberty. This belief occasioned another differentiation in Jouvenel's view of liberty: that between an economic liberty and a political liberty. Economic liberty formed the basis of self-asserted liberty by virtue of supplying the individual with a means of existence not reliant on a primary Power. In contrast, political liberty was that recognised by a primary Power regardless of the ability of the individuals possessing this liberty to actualise it. In this sense, economic and political liberty could overlap, and for Jouvenel problems occurred when this political liberty was granted to those without economic liberty, thereby making them, by default, beholden to a greater power for this liberty. Another way of viewing this distinction is that Jouvenel was asserting that there is a difference between a liberty as enforced by subsidiary power centres against the primary Power centre, and a liberty as granted by, enforced by, and only at the sufferance of, the primary Power centre. This belief led Jouvenel to see a significant divergence in the historical development of England and France. In England,

---

1 Jouvenel also offers a third kind of liberty which he believes is obtained by the existence of competing authorities: "when there are two masters, squire and state, battling for their allegiance, the intervention of Power creates for them a sort of liberty. Not, it is true, the liberty which comes from a man's own assertion of his own rights, but a poorer quality of liberty, liberty by another's intervention, than which the securitarian temper can know no other." Jouvenel, *On Power*, 344.

he believed that the middle class had formed an alliance with the aristocracy, which had lent the English state a character more conducive to a real liberty based on self-sufficiency than had the French middle class' alliance with the monarchy. The basis of this difference was that in England the aristocracy supposedly expanded the aristocratic conception of liberty to all, and so strengthened the individual's position, whilst in France it was the inferior liberty of the primary Power centre which was extended to all, and which left them in a state of being, in reality, not in possession of true liberty. Instead, they held a false liberty only by virtue of the king, or, following the French Revolution, by virtue of the central government.

We must understand how it is that Jouvenel believed that an aristocratic culture of true liberty not dependent on a primary Power centre could be maintained; at the centre of this scheme is the primacy of law. Jouvenel correctly understood that law, as understood in modern societies, is a relatively new phenomenon, and that the idea that law can be created by a sovereign legislator, as opposed to being something discovered, was alien to earlier societies. Take, for example, the Roman conception of law. For the Romans, as Jouvenel explains, law had a dual character. There was first a law which referred to the gods—*fas*—and then there was a law which referred to the relations of men to each other—*jus*. This *fas* could not be altered by man, but was something sacred to be discovered. It was not, in any sense, positive law. This continues in a different form with law in the medieval period, where divine law was not mandated by a sovereign, but instead encompassed all in society, king included. There was, therefore, no sovereignty at all in the modern sense, something we shall cover in more detail in chapter 3. Law was not something to be created, but something to be discovered, and with which to be accorded. Within this scheme, the freedom of the primary Power centre is greatly circumscribed, as it must adhere to the generally accepted laws of the order, no less than does every other section of the order. This is why medieval and early modern actors framed their claims to rights within the language of rediscovering ancient customs and law, as bizarre as this may sound to modern ears.[2] For Jouvenel,

---

2 Jouvenel describes this move from discovered law to legislation as having been accomplished in three steps: first, restating what the custom is; second, dressing

this web of law controlling all within society created the binding, shared culture which allowed for various power centres to exist, and for these individuals to live in a state of independence, and yet also a state of sociability.

Jouvenel maintained that within a society wherein law is above the primary Power centre, aristocratic conceptions of individual rights can, and did, arise from a patrician "people."[3] This is exemplified in the Greek and Roman republics which clearly form a model that Jouvenel admires. This, however, raises a problem, in that the nature of the individual in Jouvenel's work is a wholly unclear concept. This manifests in Jouvenel referring to individuals in antiquity in the same way that he refers to individuals in modernity. Surely Jouvenel cannot have envisioned the *Eupatrids* and *Patricians* of the Athenian and Roman orders as corresponding to the individual of modernity, and he gives no impression of this; however, we are still left with ambiguity on the matter. The development of the individual, as conceived by modernity, is something that we shall see in later chapters has its own unique characteristics, and it is also something which, confusingly, Jouvenel himself recognises as a rather late creation when he comments that with modernity:

> The state and the individual were just emerging triumphant
> from their long struggle waged in common against the social
> authorities, which were hateful to the one as rivals and to the
> other as tyrants.[4]

What, then, are we to make of the obvious contradiction created by both his references to the individual of antiquity and his recognition of the individual's connection to the rise of the state? Either Jouvenel has entered into a state of confusion, or he is applying the word "individual" to multiple concepts in the same way as he did with "liberty." If we assume, given Jouvenel's definitions of liberty, that he is implying that there are two forms of individual, then one type of individual would seem to be represented in the form of the aristocracy, and the other in the state-created

innovation up as a return to this custom; finally, breaking from the pretence that the innovations are ancient custom at all. Jouvenel, *On Power*, 209.

3   ibid., 249.

4   ibid., 375.

individual. This interpretation is supported by Jouvenel's own rec-ognition that in ancient republics the individuals that comprised the "people" were not women, servants, slaves, children, etc., but instead the heads of families, so that when we read that in Rome the "people" drove out the kings, what this really means is that the patricians drove out the kings.[5] In contrast, the modern individual is not an individual of the aristocracy; he is instead a *subject*, and this subject-individual is premised on a complete disregard for his ability to maintain his individuality separate from the king's, or the government's, enforcement of his rights as an individual.[6]

The subject-individual, or the individual of modernity identi-fied by Jouvenel, is an individual familiar to all. This is the indi-vidual that forms the basis of human rights, and is the individual implied by all modern liberal theory. We will explore this individ-ual in more detail in later chapters, but for now it suffices to note that this individual is premised on an atomistic and pre-societal basis, which demands that he be endowed with his characteristics irrespective of the order within which he exists. The psychological make-up of this individual, such as his desires, fears, values, and even epistemology, do not, and cannot, rely on the greater order in any way.

Given this state of affairs, the question faced by modern think-ers from the start has been why this sovereign individual was drawn into forming orders in the first place. The response to this conundrum has been the adoption of social contract theories. The story that accompanies this kind of thought follows the gener-al pattern that, in creating orders, these individuals enter into a form of contract, and supposedly grant a portion of their natu-ral (non-order-dependent), individual rights to a sovereign. This sovereign then presides over the order with its newly acquired sovereignty, thus enabling all to live in peace. What, then, is the nature of Jouvenel's aristocratic-individual? Does it have a basis different from this individual of modernity? The answers to these questions become clear when Jouvenel's own account of human order formation is presented.

---

5 Jouvenel, *On Power*, 88.
6 The articulation of this division between the individual of the aristocratic re-public and the individual of the monarchy is seen at its most vivid on pp. 90–91 of *On Power*.

In chapter IV, *The Magical Origins of Power*, we find Jouvenel's speculations as to the origins of human orders, along with his analysis of something he terms "magical Power."[7] According to Jouvenel, before the advent of kingship, "primitive peoples"[8] lived in a state of existence without a central governing apparatus. The society was not governed by men, but by "powers which overarch society"[9]—"powers" here being gods and spirits. There were no sovereign individuals or institutions as we would recognise them. In this sense, Jouvenel is perfectly correct, as noted in more recent scholarship on the nature of early kingship.[10] Within such orders, the role of the leading men of society, and even of the king, was not to create law, but to interpret the will of the gods. This overarching power can, therefore, be seen as a pattern of existence wherein society is centred around an external point, as Jouvenel articulates with his description of the Roman adherence to sacrificial ceremonies:

> Take the history of the least religious people the world has seen—the Romans: even among them, as we read, sacrifice and consultation of the auspices preceded the opening of a debate.
>
> [...]
>
> We must picture the sacrificial stone and the gathering of the Elders as forming the spiritual centre from which political decision radiated—decision which wore the dress and carried the authority of a religious oracle.[11]

Jouvenel must then explain why this form of society is created in the first place. His answer is that it is fear which drives individuals to form these societies, as he writes:

> The plumed paladin and the naked philosopher, those eighteenth–century hallucinations, have no existence for the ethnologist of today. The savage's body is, as he knows, exposed to such suffering as through the organisation of society we are spared; his soul is shaken by such terrors as would make

7 Jouvenel, *On Power*, 71.
8 ibid., 71.
9 ibid., 71.
10 Graeber and Sahlins, *On Kings*.
11 Jouvenel, *On Power*, 71.

> our most horrible nightmares seem but passing dreams. The
> reaction of the human flock to all dangers and terrors is like
> that of animals: they gather closer, they curl themselves up,
> they give each other warmth. They find in numbers the prin-
> ciple of strength and safety for themselves.[12]

Jouvenel does not expressly claim that this society is comprised of individuals, which would render the resultant society secondary to the individual, but this is the only conclusion which one can draw from his explanation. Logically, these individuals must have an individuality not predicated on society, and must merely create society out of a sort of flocking due to fear. Granted, this is not a societal formation in which the individuals fear one another, as with Thomas Hobbes' famous state of nature, but they instead fear the greater world, or the gods to whom the society sacrifices. This sacrificial centre, around which they supposedly form, is clearly not an integral element of the makeup of these pre-modern indi-viduals, and is consequent to their obviously inherent individual-ity. Jouvenel is applying modern liberal anthropology to ancient societies, and as one proceeds throughout his work this individual reappears continuously, despite Jouvenel's many claims as to the natural sociability of man.

This insistence on an individual existing separately from any given society stands at odds with the centrality of society de-manded by Jouvenel's political theory. In his historical analysis, all societies are invariably centralised. At first, these societies are centralised around a sacrificial centre, and later, after this central-ity has been appropriated by tribal chiefs, it is the kings, and still later the democratic state, which take up this position in society. This creates a problem for Jouvenel in that, since his historical account relies on the modern individual as an unrecognised as-sumption, he must explain this perennial pattern of centrality ac-cording to an individualist model, which means he is forced to develop convoluted and unsatisfactory explanations for a pattern integral to his model. Take, for example, chapter I, *Of Civil Obe-dience*, where Jouvenel attempts to account for the obedience that society grants to governments, and, therefore, the continuance of this centralised structure, as simply "habit." Of course, this habit

12 Jouvenel, *On Power*, 69.

cannot explain how government expands because this introduces something contrary to habit; here, Jouvenel resorts to a further explanation in the form of "reason," which enables government to make claims as to its beneficial nature, as he writes:

> Force alone can establish Power, habit alone can keep it in being, but to expand it must have credit—a thing which, even in its earlier life, it finds useful and has generally received in practice. As a description of Power, rather than as a definition, we may now call it a standing corporation, which is obeyed from habit, has the means of physical compulsion, and is kept in being partly by the view taken of its strength, partly by the faith that it rules as of right (in other words, its legitimacy), and partly by the hope of its beneficence.[13]

So, we could see this as a multi-layered explanation. First, force uses "fear" as the binding agent of society (just as, earlier, fear had supposedly created the sacrificial orders), then "habit" replaces this "fear" (which implies an unexplained inertia implicit in society).

Does Jouvenel's explanation based on an individualistic society and an individualistic psychology adequately explain "there being in every society a centre of control"? I believe it does not, because there is no conceivable reason why a centralised Power would be maintained in all instances, and across all times, on the basis presented by Jouvenel. At this point, the possibility suggests itself that perhaps we can agree with Jouvenel as to the importance of this centrality and pursue a different and far more radical interpretation of its nature. To do so, however, requires that we take an approach quite alien to modern political thought. If we discount the modern individual and begin solely from the Jouvenelian model of centrality, then we would, in taking such an approach, be proceeding from the middle of our inquiry. This is alien to modern political theory because it is usually accepted that one must begin from foundationalist first principles when developing a model, and must then explain complex systems on this basis. This is evidenced by the prevalence and esteem enjoyed by political science with its adherence to methodological individualism, a characteristic which we shall encounter in more detail in

13 Jouvenel, *On Power*, 25.

chapter 8.

Taking Jouvenel's model of centrality as hypothetically correct, we shall develop first principles in an Aristotelian/Thomistic manner, which will bring us into epistemological dispute with modernity. That we will enter into an epistemological dispute may at first seem to be a non sequitur, but as we proceed it will become apparent that political models of human orders are intimately entwined with epistemology for the simple reason that epistemology turns on the question of what constitutes a justifiable source of knowledge. Can the individual, as conceived by philosophy, rely on the authority of others in the form of accepted thought or tradition? Modernity's answer has been that the radical individual can, and should, do without any reliance on external sources of influence. Such an epistemology requires a human agent who can begin from nothing and nowhere, and can then engage in the process of thinking from this vacuum. We see such an individual in the form of the Cartesian individual reasoning from a position of radical doubt, an individual which heralded the beginning of modern philosophy.

Beginning from this middle is something which, therefore, requires that the reader take the model presented in chapter 1 as *prima facie* correct, and then, from their comprehension of the model as explained thus far, that they follow the dialectical development of first principles in accordance with, and as comprehensible only within, the logic of the model. Does, then, the individual of modernity, which fills the role of a first principle for political science, follow from the Jouvenelian model of centrality? As we proceed it will become clear that it categorically does not. So, what can the consistent centrality of human orders tell us about human nature? To answer this question requires that we find an anthropological account which accords with such a pattern. What would an anthropology in accordance with the Jouvenelian model look like? Possible alternatives include the mimetic anthropology of René Girard and the linguistic developments made by Eric Gans, which we can briefly review.

In the anthropology inaugurated by René Girard,[14] the sacrifi-

---

14   Girard first introduced his theory of memetic desire in René Girard, *Deceit, Desire, and the Novel: Self and Other in Literary Structure* (Baltimore: Johns Hopkins University Press, 2010).

cial order of society, which Jouvenel himself recognised as key to early human societal formation in the form of magical Power, is not the creation of human individuals and separate from them, but an integral part of them. In the work of Girard, the move from a pre-human society of mimetic beings to a (still fundamentally mimetic) human society was the result of a mimetic crisis. Girard's theory is based upon the observation that humans are, therefore, inescapably mimetic. The nature of desire is such that it is not, as assumed by modern liberal anthropology, inherent to the individual and sovereign—the individual does not face society with his own desires to then be satisfied within a marketplace, but learns these desires from others. For Girard, this mimetic desire is a source of conflict and tension within societies, and it is mitigated through the act of focusing the cumulative mimetic desires of a society on a single individual who becomes a scapegoat. In the act of killing this scapegoat, the individuals become aware of both the violence towards the scapegoat blamed for this collective animosity and the dissipation of this animosity. The sacrificial scapegoat becomes at once the cause of all the society's ills, and also its salvation from these ills. The scapegoat then becomes a sacred object.

In the work of Eric Gans, this model is presented as an explanation for the origin of language, where the creation of the first sign, and therefore the beginning of language, results from an abortive ostensive gesture in the process of mimetic descent on (most likely) an animal which has been killed. This abortive sign is hypothesised to be a representation of the object at the centre of the group's collective mimetic desire. In both intensely mimetically desiring the object, yet also being aware of the violence that will ensue if members of the group all descend on the object, the sign takes on a sacred nature. It is in the wake of the collective attention created by this event that language is first generated from an ostensive syntactical form which has subsequently evolved into a number of further forms, these being the imperative and then the declarative. Thus, in this scheme, language is a product of mimetic desire, is generative, and as in Girard's account, presupposes an anthropological model implying that humanity has resulted from a process of shared attention around a centre external to any of the individuals. The human individual of modernity makes no sense within such a system, since everything from language to thought (which always occurs within a language) is premised on a mimetic relationship that is incomplete without reference to this shared external centre.[15]

The reader may raise issues with hypothetically entertaining such anthropological accounts, but before dismissing them we must acknowledge that these accounts present far fuller explanations of human orders, and that they provide grounds for a deeper understanding than that of the modern anthropology of atomistic individuals possessing a radical subjectivity. We can go even further and claim that this modern anthropology is not only incompatible with the Jouvenelian model, but that its development is, in actuality, explainable by the model as a side effect of the Jouvenelian conflicts which have occurred within the Western world. To this end, we shall first review the development of theories of political legitimacy and sovereignty in light of the Jouvenelian model in order to provide a context within which the individual of the modern model can be fully understood.

15 For the latest work by Eric Gans dealing with the generative nature of language, see Eric Gans, *The Origin of Language: A New Edition* (New York: Spuyten Duyvil Publishing, 2019).

III

THE ARRIVAL OF SOVEREIGNTY

In standard histories of political theory, one gets the impression that the history of political theories of legitimacy can be cleanly separated into two epochs. There is a pre-modern period, which has little relevance to anyone but historians, and then there is a modern period, which has broken so forcefully from the former that it represents something of a miracle. Within this framework, monarchical divine right theorists are usually assigned the role of representatives of the pre-modern world, typically in the shape of Sir Robert Filmer who has become little more than a foil for the advocates of supposedly modern consensual theories of legitimacy, as typified by John Locke. In modern thought, these theorists of consensual political orders are presented as the harbingers of a democratic (and, therefore, of a non-centralised) modernity.[1] Subsequently, democracy and monarchy have been understood as so radically different in form that the decisions and actions of Henry IV, the Holy Roman Emperor, or of Louis XI of France, are thought to have no relevance to modern political theory. From the angle of the Jouvenelian model, this entire framework of un-

1   For a review of this form of historiography relating to Filmer and modernity, see Cesare Cuttica, "Sir Robert Filmer (1588–1653) and the Condescension of Posterity: Historiographical Interpretations," *Intellectual History Review*, Vol. 21, Issue 2 (2011): 195–208. https://doi.org/10.1080/17496977.2011.574345.

derstanding is radically misguided. To understand how this is so, we can trace the origins of consensual theories of legitimacy past their claimed beginnings in the 16th century. To do this, we must first return to the divine right monarchical governance theories in order to understand the place of each in relation to the other.

In this task, the first important point we encounter is that theories of divine right sovereignty are not, in fact, particularly old concepts, nor were they, oddly enough, intrinsically linked to monarchy. In fact, divine right sovereignty is a relatively new development, and its origins can be traced to the rise of the papacy. It is in the development of *Plenitudo Potestatis*[2]—a concept which was, by the 13th century,[3] extensively used by the Popes to assert their pre-eminence over secular rulers—that we can first see the divine right theory taking shape. At this point it is obviously not a monarchical concept; neither is it one which can be said to describe sovereignty in a strict sense, since the concept of sovereignty, with its connection to the creation of law, was yet to be developed. It is also important to note that this concept asserts that the Pope's authority derives from his position as the Vicar of Christ; this renders legitimacy unidirectional, and places the origin of legitimacy outside the order in question.[4] This development did not happen in a vacuum, and as such, we must attend to its circumstances. In doing so, we find that the assertion of *Plenitudo Potestatis* followed in the wake of a great centralisation of Church control in the hands of the papacy.

As with the history of monarchy, the ordinary reader may lack

2   *Plenitudo Potestatis* is the concept that the Pope's authority is supreme within the Catholic Church, and which later came to be employed in claims to supremacy over the secular sphere as well. While it does not translate directly to modern conceptions of sovereignty as developed by Jean Bodin, the comparison is an easy one to draw. See William D. McCready, "Papal *Plenitudo Potestatis* and the Source of Temporal Authority in Late Medieval Papal Hierocratic Theory," *Speculum*, 48, no. 4, (October 1973): 654–74. https://doi.org/10.2307/2856222.

3   Brian Tierney, *Foundations of the Conciliar Theory: The Contribution of the Medieval Canonists from Gratian to the Great Schism* (Cambridge: Cambridge University Press, 1955), 144–49.

4   It seems that Pope Innocent III, in particular, was exceptionally innovative in this regard, even asserting that his power was drawn from his position as Vicar of God, a point which was developed by the canonist Hostiensis. See K. Pennington, "Law, Legislative Authority, and Theories of Government, 1150–1300," in *The Cambridge History of Medieval Political Thought, c.350–c.1450*, ed. J.H. Burns (Cambridge: University Press, 1988), 424–53.

knowledge as to the development of the papacy, and so may not be aware that the current structure of the Church as organised around the papacy dates only to the 11th century. Church reformers had been working towards such a state of affairs for some time, and with the Gregorian Reforms this work was carried to fruition. Henry III, the Holy Roman Emperor, became a major sponsor of reforming actors from around 1044 for reasons less to do with theology and more to do with the necessities of governance. Henry III seems to have been closely concerned with papal matters as a means to secure his crown, nominating a number of bishops of German origin who would, in turn, legitimise the emperor. These reformers opposed simony—the sale of Church offices—and as a result, they were opponents of the current papal incumbents; thus, they formed a natural alliance with the emperor. With the changes in the political landscape following the death of Henry III, the papacy fell out of the control of the Holy Roman Empire, and it began to act with some autonomy due to having alternative sources of support, such as Duke Godfrey in Tuscany, or the Normans who had become a power in southern Italy.[5]

It was in this power vacuum that Gregory VII became Pope in 1073, and it was he who would give his name to the famous Gregorian Reforms, with his major sponsor being the court of Matilda of Tuscany.[6] At this point, the reformers, whom the Holy Roman Empire had initially sponsored into prominence, excommunicated the Holy Roman Emperor, Henry IV. This undermined Henry's legitimacy, predicated as it was on his being the ruler of the *Holy* Roman Empire. That Henry was brought to the point of grovelling for repentance from Gregory at the gates of Cannossa Castle, the castle of Matilda of Tuscany, speaks to the papacy's success in this dynamic.

It was within this context that Gregory VII went on to assert superiority over the secular realm, and it was within this context that the Popes took on a divine right justification which can be seen clearly in the *Dictus Papae*.[7] In this document, we find the

---

5 For an account of the changes that occurred during the period in question, and the likely incentives for the various actors to act as they did, see Colin Morris, *The Papal Monarchy: The Western Church from 1050 to 1250* (Oxford: Clarendon Press, 1989), 83–97.

6 Morris, *The Papal Monarchy*, 52.

7 Ernest F. Henderson, "The Dictate of the Pope," in *Select Historical Documents*

Pope declaring not only that Church appointments were his sole prerogative, but also that he had the right to depose emperors, that the Church was founded by God alone, and that the Pope can be judged by no human individual. By the time we get to Innocent III and the canonist Hostiensis, the concept of *Plenitudo Potestatis* had been fully developed into a sophisticated version of divine right authority, wherein the Pope is under the authority of God alone.[8]

Those who opposed these claims, be they theologians or apologists of secular authorities, responded in a way which is key to the theory contained in this work: they simply altered who the ultimate receiver of authority was. We will find this internal redirection of a tradition repeated in many different areas of political thought as we proceed through this work, and its importance cannot be overstated. The means by which Protestant reformers, in particular, managed to achieve this was first, by focusing on the inherent division of governance accepted by authorities in the Christian world order—secular vs. ecclesiastical—and then by focusing on a specific interpretation of this division's implications.

At this point, we must note that the nature of this division was not the same as it is now. Clearly demarcated secular and religious realms did not exist; the idea of there being some space within life separable from Christian doctrine was unknown. Therefore, when we see the conflict between the emperors and the Church, we must understand that while this has an echo in the modern concept of the division of church and state, it is not the same thing. The emperor, and later the kings of Europe, saw themselves as all part of the same Christian order as the Church and the Popes. This is what makes the concept of divine right kingship possible; we are yet to meet the modern invention of the concept of religion, and the belief that some aspect of the world can be secular and without overall meaning.

Within this shared Christian order, dissenting voices in opposition to the papacy latched onto the Augustinian division of the City of Man and the City of God. This division, articulated in Augustine's *The City of God*, called upon the faithful to turn their

of the Middle Ages (London: George Bell and Sons, 1910), 366–67.

8   Pennington, "Law, Legislative Authority, and Theories of Government," 424–53.

eyes away from the transitory world (the City of Man) and to-wards heaven (the City of God). These dissenting voices claimed that the Church had strayed from the apostolic truth of the early Church, and had become corrupted by its involvement in earthly affairs. According to these schemes, the Church was supposed to be concerned expressly with the City of God—the saving of souls; but this left open the issue of governance of the fallen realm of the City of Man. The obvious solution was to claim that monar-chical authorities should be left to this task, and they were able to employ biblical references in support of this position.[9] This move gave divine right sanction in matters of governance not to the papacy, which the reformers could point out was an institution not mentioned in the Bible (and which, in their view, should not be involved in earthly matters in any case), but to kings, to whom we are instructed to give allegiance in many biblical passages.[10]

The Church's supposed failure to live up to these exacting stan-dards of holiness in the eyes of the reformers, and its failure to reform accordingly, led the most ardent reformers to turn to mo-narchical authorities to forcefully reform the Church for its own good.[11] Such a message was, understandably, warmly welcomed by secular authorities as it justified their expansion of power and expropriation of property at the Church's expense. The implica-tions this has for ethics, theology, philosophy, and other elements of thought which derive from these sources, will be discussed in greater detail in later chapters, but for now we can concentrate on the influence of structural conflict on the success of these tradi-tions. The most fruitful way to do this is to examine the context within which the major thinkers rose to prominence, and how they were able to obtain such great influence. In short, we can ask if the success of these reformers was connected to some sort of truth value, or if it was a side effect of conflict.

9   Romans 13:1–7 seems to have been particularly relevant to the reformers.
10   It is notable that the earlier Gregorian Reforms had been made under the banner of restoring a primitive apostolic order to the Church as well. See Morris, *The Papal Monarchy,* 28–33.
11   The theological concepts developed by this cast of characters included such innovations as the invisible Church of the Elect, predestination, and justifica-tion by faith alone. These doctrines can all be simplified to an assertion that the Church, as an institution, is unfit to make judgements on doctrinal matters, and that this doctrine can be adjudicated by the individual simply referring to the Bible.

One of the first clear examples we have of the developing relationship between the monarchical courts of Europe and re-forming actors is seen in the travails of William of Ockham who, following a dispute with papal authorities, fled the Pope's court in Avignon with Michael of Cesena. Both men ultimately found refuge in the court of Louis IV of Bavaria, who had been excommunicated in 1324. Here they enjoyed the company of Marsilius of Padua.[12] The sources of Ockham's dispute with Pope John XII are various and rooted in theological arguments primarily over the status of evangelical poverty, but this is of secondary importance to the value that the secular court which sheltered him found in his rejection of papal superiority. As with the later Protestants, Ockham was typical in advocating for the divine right of secular authorities to govern, and in rejecting the authority of the papacy to (generally) intervene outside of spiritual matters.[13]

Another example of this developing relationship is that of the morning star of the Reformation, John Wycliffe, to John of Gaunt, 1st Duke of Lancaster and uncle of King Richard II, and to Richard II himself.[14] Wycliffe's theological claims are not significantly different from Ockham's in that he claimed that the Church was too involved with secular matters, was neglecting its spiritual role, and was, as a result, straying from the true apostolic path. In Wycliffe's view also, secular authorities were encouraged to assist the Church in purifying itself for its own good.[15] As with Ockham, Wycliffe's appeal to an apostolic vision of the Church, as against the papal dominated Church, contained specific elements of support for monarchical rule which were of value to sec-

12 Marsilius, the author of *Defensor Pacis*, had also earned the enmity of the papacy for his defence of the primacy of the monarchy, and was, therefore, unsurprisingly welcome at the court along with Ockham. Jouvenel is rather dismissive of Marsilius' quasi-popular-sovereignty argument in *Defensor Pacis*, writing that it "makes no attempt to conceal its lack of disinterestedness. The point of it is, as any child could see, that the multitude has been endowed with this majestic authority merely that it may pass it on, stage by stage, to a despot." Jouvenel, *On Power*, 33. The despot referenced being, of course, Louis of Bavaria, Marsilius' patron.
13 For an extensive overview of the various interpretations of Ockham's thought, see Arthur Stephen McGrade, *The Political Thought of William of Ockham: Personal and Institutional Principles* (Cambridge: Cambridge University Press, 2002).
14 See John Neville Figgis, "Wycliffe and King Richard II," in *The Divine Right of Kings* (Cambridge: University Press, 1914), 66–80.
15 For a review of John Wycliffe's political thought, see John Lowrie Daley, *The Political Theory of John Wyclif* (Chicago: Loyola Press, 1962).

ular authorities, and which seem better able to predict his success than does the theological value of his claims. That Richard II, like his uncle, would later go on to support Wycliffe and the Lollards is not surprising. He even had a number of Lollards in his court.[16]

Wycliffe's thought would even prove influential in Bohemian circles due to a connection between the two kingdoms created by Richard II's wife, Ann, the daughter of the Bohemian King Charles IV. In addition, there was also a connection in the form of an exchange of thought between the University of Prague and the University of Oxford, a conduit whereby Wycliffe's beliefs became institutionalised in Bohemia. His theological thought would go on to play a role in the conflicts between the laity and the ecclesiastical orders there, with Jan Hus, the famed leader of the Bohemian Reformation, being especially influenced by him.[17]

This pattern of behaviour is not exhausted by these examples. Martin Luther, the most famous of all Protestant reformers, was himself sponsored by a secular patron in the form of the Elector of Saxony, Frederick III. Not only did Frederick provide continual protection from papal authorities, but he also provided the institutional infrastructure within which Luther operated in the form of the University of Wittenberg.[18] At any point in time, Frederick had the ability to remove Luther and hand him over to papal authorities; instead, he provided the institutions and resources that enabled Luther to flourish. As with Ockham and Wycliffe, Luther, a militant Augustinian, claimed that obedience was owed to secular authorities in accordance with the Bible.[19] Luther, working from the division of the City of God and the City of Man, also promulgated his well-known system of "two governments"[20] which followed the same pattern as Wycliffe's and Ockham's favouring of secular authorities. To this end, he made direct appeal to the German nobility to enact the necessary reforms, and so

16 See Richard Rex, "The Early Diffusion of Lollardy: Lollardy and Patronage," in *The Lollards* (Basingstoke: Palgrave, 2002), 61–64.
17 For a review of the historical connection between the University of Prague and Oxford, see O. Odlozilnik, "Wycliffe's Influence on Eastern and Central Europe," *The Slavonic and East European Review*, VII, No. 21 (1929): 634–48.
18 Eric Leland Saak, *Luther and the Reformation of the Later Middle Ages* (Cambridge: Cambridge University Press, 2017), 203.
19 R.W. and A.J. Carlyle, *A History of Mediaeval Political Theory in the West, Vol VI: Political Theory from 1300 to 1600* (London: Blackwood, 1936), 272.
20 ibid., 273–74.

cleanse the Church of involvement in secular matters.[21] He even boasted that his support of secular authorities surpassed that of all his predecessors.[22]

From these many examples, we can clearly see the role of Jouvenel's mechanism of centres of power supporting dissenting thought because of its use in structural conflict. The protection of schismatic sects, and the promotion of what Jouvenel called "the most ignorant of the preachers,"[23] becomes an obvious means of extending the power of the centres in question at the expense of other centres of power—in this case, at the expense of ecclesiastical centres of power. This is supported by William Cavanaugh's observation that the Reformation failed in those states that were advanced in the state's absorption of ecclesiastical power.[24] The secular authorities had already wrested sufficient control away from the Church to render unnecessary the support of Protestant theological claims, which demonstrates the direct connection between structural conflict and the progression of ideas.

With the monarchs having obtained a great deal of power under the banner of these divine right theories developed by Protestant reformers to vanquish the Church, the opponents of the centralising monarchy needed to formulate new ideological rejections. Here, we can see that those patterns of thought brought into prominence are, again, chosen for their service to the needs of specific centres of power, and yet again, represent an alteration of an already existing tradition. The main actors in this endeavour were papal supporters, parliamentarians, and Huguenot theolo-

21 "...the Christian nobility should rise up against the Pope as a common enemy and destroyer of Christianity, for the sake of the salvation of the poor souls that such tyranny must ruin." Martin Luther, "An Open Letter to the Christian Nobility Concerning the Reform of the Christian Estate (1520)," in *Works of Martin Luther: With Introductions and Notes, Volume II* (Philadelphia: A.J. Holman Company, 1915), 29.

22 Alasdair C. MacIntyre, *A Short History of Ethics: A History of Moral Philosophy from the Homeric Age to the Twentieth Century* (New York: Simon & Schuster, 1996), 122.

23 Jouvenel, *On Power,* 178.

24 "It is unarguably the case that the reinforcement of ecclesiastical difference in early modern Europe was largely a project of state-building elites. As G.R. Elton bluntly puts it, 'The Reformation maintained itself wherever the lay power (prince or magistrates) favoured it; it could not survive wherever the authorities decided to suppress it.'" William T. Cavanaugh, *The Myth of Religious Violence: Secular Ideology and the Roots of Modern Conflict* (Oxford: Oxford University Press, 2009), 168.

gians. The goal of papal supporters was to turn the monarchical claim of divine right on its head by latching onto the historically elective nature of monarchies. To this end, at the request of Pope Paul V, Francisco Suarez penned *Defensio Fidei Catholicae* (1613) as a refutation of King James I's divine right theories contained in such works as *The True Law of Free Monarchies* (1598). This protracted theological debate between the king and the Pope also involved Cardinal Robert Bellarmine, another theologian who asserted the consensual nature of monarchy. The argument adopted by Suarez was the natural-law-based claim that "man is by his nature free and subject to no one, save only to the Creator, so that human sovereignty is contrary to the order of nature and involves tyranny."[25] On this basis, he concluded that political authority initially rests with the people, and that political authority is, consequently, a product of the consent of these individuals. This is yet another alteration of the initial receiver of divine right, and not a rejection of the divine right tradition. It should also be noted that this idea of consensual governance, whilst being new in its Christian divine right setting, was not an invention of Suarez's, but was actually developed from Roman law. In fact, a closer look at the whole body of social contract theory reveals that even the Romans were not innovators in this regard; we can even find such thought among the ancient Greeks.[26]

The other direction from which this social contract theorising developed was from French Huguenot thinkers who, like the Church and its supporters, were in a position of conflict with a monarchical centre of Power. With the Huguenots, the situation is complicated by the shifting nature of conflicts in 16th century France, where, at times, the Huguenots were supporters of monarchy, and at other times, its greatest enemy. It was during a period in which the Huguenots had become estranged from the French court that they began to formulate theories of popular consent.[27] The first stage in this process was the development of

25 "De Legibus" III, 1.1, *Selection from Three Works of Francisco Suarez, S.J., Volume Two* (Oxford: Clarendon Press, 1944), 363.

26 A number of writers have noted the historical repetition of social contract thinking. D.G. Ritchie provides a very informative paper on the issue in "Contributions to the History of Social Contract Theory," *Political Science Quarterly*, Vol. 6, No. 4 (December 1891): 656–676. http://www.jstor.org/stable/2139203.

27 That this occurred after the Huguenots had fallen out of favour with Queen

the doctrine that lesser officials in the monarchical structure were invested with the right to disobey the monarch. This initial step in the breach of the king's direct divine right subsequently developed into a fully fledged doctrine of consent of the people.[28]

This pattern of structural conflict preceding theory is even more blatant in the constitutional legal tradition developed by supporters of the English Parliament in the 17th century. The centralising efforts of monarchs in England, such as those of Charles I, had caused a great deal of friction, leading to a broad rejection of their new claims to sovereignty. A key part of this sovereignty was the status of law, and on this front, both sides had a basis for their specific claims; however, this debate did not proceed in anything like an orderly fashion. The king's supporters pointed towards the origin of parliamentary laws in the form of the king, while the parliamentary opponents insisted on a historical interpretation whereby constitutional law was simply the recording of rights of ancient origin and which predated the king—this rather gives away the nature of these theoretical constructs as being secondary to immediate practical needs. This pattern of centralisation and opposition to centralisation gave rise to similar movements in other kingdoms of the time (most notably Francois Hotman in France), as noted by J.G.A. Pocock who saw that these thinkers were driven to a:

> ...kind of historical obscurantism—compelled to attribute their liberties to more and more remote and mythical periods in the effort to prove them independent of the will of the king.[29]

Elizabeth de Medici, and in the wake of the events of the St. Bartholomew massacre, is symptomatic of the nature of political thought following power-driven necessity.

28 For accounts of the development of Huguenot thought on the justifiability of resistance against a monarch, see Mack P. Holt, "The Rhetoric of Resistance: The Unmasking of the Body Politic, 1574–1584," in *The French Wars of Religion, 1562–1629* (Cambridge: Cambridge University Press, 2007), 99–122. Also see J.H.M. Salmon, "The Development of Political Ideas," in *The French Wars of Religion: How Important Were Religious Factors?* ed. J.H.M. Salmon (Lexington: D.C. Heath and Company, 1967), 76–79.

29 J.G.A. Pocock, *The Ancient Constitution and the Feudal Law: A Study of English Thought in the Seventeenth Century* (Cambridge: Cambridge University Press, 1987), 17.

While, in one sense, these legal thinkers were wrong in their claims that the existing legal system did not derive from monarchical authority, and that the rights enjoyed by Parliament did not depend on the king, in another sense, they were correctly articulating that the order of Charles I and his contemporaries was a new development, and that law in its original form was not an emanation from the king. This rather clumsy legalistic refutation of centralisation was complemented by the equally clumsy theological and philosophical thought of the divine right social contract theorists of the 17th century who continued the Catholic and Huguenot trend of appealing to a mythical pre-political state of nature. Foremost among these theorists were those harbingers of modern political theory, John Locke and Thomas Hobbes, whose tradition of thought still dominates the modern world.

The confusing nature of this body of thought—one which has kept political theorists engaged in convoluted and inconclusive debate for centuries—is seen, from a structural angle, to result from it having to accomplish two divergent goals at the same time. In the first instance, this social contract theorising was required to undermine monarchical claims to divine right sovereignty. For this purpose, the claim of the people as the determinants of divine right was employed, and the king was supplanted in the hierarchy.[30] The second use to which these social contract theories were put was in justifying a new political order of a centralised nature, and as such, we get social contract theories of sovereignty. At this point, the concept of sovereignty in its modern form becomes unavoidably entangled with issues of political legitimacy, and the reason for this is quite clearly explained by Jouvenel. As Jouvenel notes, sovereignty fundamentally depends on a conception of society as comprised of individuals, so that:

> This purely nominalist conception of society renders intelligible the notion of sovereignty. Society consists only of asso-

---

30 Jouvenel notes the manner in which theories of sovereignty have been disputes over the initial receivers of authority from God when he comments that popular sovereignty is the result of "taking away from the three following expressions the first one—God the author of Power, the people who confer Power, the rulers who receive it and exercise. It is affirmed, after this abstraction, that Power belongs to society in full fee simple and is then conferred by it alone on its rulers. That is the theory of popular sovereignty." Jouvenel, *On Power*, 33.

ciated men, whose disassociation is always possible.[31]

And it is just such a conception that was bequeathed by the theories of political legitimacy that derived from a specific Christian tradition. It is, therefore, unsurprising that we find Jean Bodin developing the first elaboration of sovereignty in the midst of the burgeoning Protestant body of thought of the France of his time. Instead of engaging in a discussion as to a true singular definition of sovereignty, something which has eluded all thinkers on the topic, it is far more helpful to approach the issue from the angle of centralisation. As with divine right conceptions of authority, the concept of sovereignty observably followed in the wake of centralisation and individualisation, and varies in its precise meaning according to the demands of the different centres of power and of the opponents of centralisation.

If we follow the argument that the Catholic Church blazed the trail for the concept of sovereignty in the form of *Plenitudo Potestatis*, we will have no problem connecting this to the new centralisation of the papacy. If, as more generally argued, we can only apply such a concept to thinkers from Bodin onwards, then we still have the same underlying cause. Here, the concept is required not by the papacy's centralisation, but by the centralisation of the various kings of France, and again, just as with the papacy, this centralisation of monarchical infrastructure is a new development. Without this centralisation, it is hard to envision Bodin's concept being formulated. We can see this by considering what exactly is required for Bodin's formulation of sovereignty. First and foremost, there must be a clear single body at the centre of the order which is independent of all others, and which operates within a set geographical area. In earlier thought, such a monopolistic entity was not envisioned because authority was fragmented and dispersed, and it was possible to speak of many sovereigns, as Dieter Grimm writes:

> Because, in the Middle Ages, such positions of power were not held by a single person, but were distributed territorially and functionally among many mutually independent holders, sovereignty could be linked only with individual powers.

31 Jouvenel, *On Power*, 45.

As a result, "sovereignty" described not an abstract but a concrete position of power, and many "sovereigns" coexisted on one and the same territory. "Sovereignty" was not a unified concept, but a plural one. Because it built upon individual powers, the characteristic of being sovereign did not suffer from the fact that its possessor was subordinate to a higher holder in regard to other powers. One could only be relatively, not absolutely, sovereign.[32]

Second, there must be a centralised and monopolistic legal system which can create law. Finally, the only law to which this sovereign is subject must be the "Law of God and nature" which was "deconfessionalized" so that it was not to be interpreted by the Catholic Church.[33] All of these features are the product of monarchical centralisation at the expense of the Church.

The exact nature of Bodin's sovereignty then undergoes significant changes dependent on time, place, and political expediency. These changes go hand in hand with the changes to divine right theory. At one point, the king is sovereign, but then this is supplanted by the claim that the people, comprised of individuals, are sovereign (which really meant that Parliament was sovereign). These individuals then grant the role of sovereign to a king, or to a centralised government, at which point the people are still sovereign, or they have alienated this sovereignty—it varies depending on the thinker. The plasticity of this concept, and the tendency of its definition to follow in the wake of whichever centre of power prevails, becomes quite evident when the example of popular sovereignty in early American history is reviewed.

The original binding document of the United States of America was the Articles of Confederation of 1781 which was considered an international treaty between the original thirteen states that had rebelled. In Article II, it is asserted that:

> Each state retains its sovereignty, freedom, and independence, and every Power, Jurisdiction and right, which is not by this confederation expressly delegated to the United States, in Congress assembled.

32 Dieter Grimm, *Sovereignty: The Origin and Future of a Political and Legal Concept* (New York: Columbia University Press, 2015), 14.
33 ibid., 22.

This understanding of sovereignty undergoes a drastic change by the time we get to the Constitution of 1787 by which point the Federalists were seeking an increased centralisation of the federal structure. Theory followed political need, and as a result, the solution that was hit upon is very obvious from a Jouvenelian angle: an appeal to the people was made at the expense of the intermediary states, and James Madison invented a "sovereign American people" to overcome the "sovereign states."[34] The Constitution, which replaced the Articles of Confederation, then contained no mention of state sovereignty, and instead opens with the famous phrase "*We the People* of the United States," which is in stark contrast to the "we, the undersigned Delegates of the States" of the Articles of Confederation. As Grimm notes:

> "We the People of the United States" was revolutionary in a dual sense: "We the People" rather than "We the Government," and "We the People" rather than "We the States."[35]

The political expediency of developing these theories of popular sovereignty to facilitate centralisation unavoidably necessitates a further concept: the individual that comprises the people. And so, we can now turn our attention to the connection between this development of political theory and the individual of modernity.

---

34 Grimm, *Sovereignty*, 38.
35 ibid., 38.

IV

THE INDIVIDUAL

THE individual in the modern sense, as Charles Taylor notes, "had a beginning in time and space and may have an end,"[1] and within the Jouvenelian model the link between the advancement of specific political theories of legitimacy and the structures of authority which support them comes into focus. One of the simplest ways we can draw attention to this link is by asking when specific developments in the concept of the individual came into prominence. If, just as with the theories of sovereignty and legitimacy in chapter 3, we can trace the development of the concept of the individual to specific political conflicts, then we will have strong support for the claim that the individual is a Jouvenelian structural phenomenon.

Previously, we noted that theories of political sovereignty, as well as the theological developments which brought them into being, possess unmistakable connections to the success of centralising structures. In the case of theories of legitimacy, this mechanism yielded divine right theories of governance—be they monarchical divine right theories, or theories of the consent of the governed (a governed mass who had themselves been imbued with divine right)—which served the needs of specific power configurations. These theories of legitimacy not only supported

1 Charles Taylor, *Sources of the Self: The Making of the Modern Identity* (Cambridge: Harvard University Press, 1989), 111.

the specific power centres which embraced them, but also worked to undermine competitors within the logic of the Jouvenelian dynamic. In the Western world, this dynamic involved monarchical support for theological accounts of Christianity with an Augustinian and Franciscan hue that, in many ways, were inimical to papal, but in accord with monarchical, claims to supremacy in the secular realm. With monarchical sponsorship, certain aspects of this apostolic theological view were emphasised in the service of the monarchical authorities, including the creation of the modern secular/sacred dichotomy in favour of the monarchy, and the ultimate rejection of the concrete Catholic Church in favour of the invisible Church of the Elect. Later, this process continued at the behest of the English Parliament, most notably with the elevation of the people above King Charles I, which meant, by extension, the elevation of *the representatives* of the people, who were, unsurprisingly, the Parliament. This was a usurpation of the divine right of the monarch by way of the people who were now established as the conduit of God's authority to govern.

The selection of these theological accounts to legitimise specific power structures meant that various additional anthropological positions had to be developed and elaborated to accord with them. Asserting that authority flows from God via the Pope requires one array of epistemological, ethical, and anthropological positions; authority flowing through the king and his own specific church requires another; authority flowing through the people requires yet another. The flourishing of this or that account of anthropology was intimately connected to the fortunes of the sponsoring power within a given power structure.

The models of political legitimacy that culminated in popular sovereignty demonstrably led to an increased focus on the people, and, by extension, the individual, as a point of reference for political thought. In the first case, the development of divine right theories of authority presupposed that authority must be granted externally by divine intervention from God. This, as Charles Taylor astutely notes, implies that authority is not natural to man.[2] The

2 "Divine right was a quintessentially modern doctrine, unlike previous mediaeval doctrines of the divine constitution of authority. Divine right assumed atomism; that is, it took for granted that there were no natural relations of authority among men, and it then argued that only a special grant of divine power to kings could avoid the chaos of anarchy. The earlier doctrines had assumed that human

Christian tradition happened to be exceptionally accommodating to such an interpretation, as Christianity indeed contains strains which point towards man, in some sense, originating from a state without authority. Larry Siedentop, in *Inventing the Individual: The Origins of Western Liberalism*, has provided a compelling history of the individual which points towards Christianity and the Church being key actors in the process of Jouvenelian centralisation as a result of employing such a Christian anthropology.[3] This raises interesting questions about the historical development and success of Christianity. If we apply the Jouvenelian model, we can even observe the early Church being shaped by the Roman emperors. It appears that these emperors played a definitive role in determining which Christian theological developments constituted the overall form of Christianity, and the evidence points towards the selection of individualising theological models in order to assist imperial authority.[4] This practice of wielding a universalised Christian individual in disputes over governance did not end with the collapse of the Roman Empire, but on the contrary, continued in the new Germanic kingdoms that formed in Western Europe following its collapse. Here, claims of the Christian individual were invoked against the new structures of the invaders, often in alliance with the Germanic kings presiding over these very same structures, as a means to break down the clans.[5]

communities had authority, and they invoked God's endorsement of the political dispositions made of this authority, whatever they might be—republican or monarchical. The seventeenth–century doctrine started from atomist premises, and it required God's intervention specifically establishing kings as his lieutenants on earth." Taylor, *Sources of the Self*, 195.

3 Larry Siedentop, *Inventing the Individual: The Origins of Western Liberalism* (Cambridge: Belknap Press of Harvard University Press, 2014).

4 Siedentop notes that Christian theological debates in the Fifth Century seem to have led to the "conclusion that the new moral beliefs entailed equal subjection to a central government, that is, to Rome's imperial majesty. This conclusion was parasitic on monotheism. It likened the imperial role to that of the divine ruler of the universe. The emperors' role provided a foretaste of the role of the Godhead, linking every person directly to the font of authority. Intermediaries became suspect. The cult of the ancient family, the association of citizens in the polis, local notables: these could no longer legitimately interpose themselves into the only relationship which had a divine sanction. Humans, despite their manifold inherited social roles, were becoming individuals, each deemed to have a soul. The ancient vision of hierarchy, social as well as natural, was fading." Siedentop, *Inventing the Individual*, 91.

5 Siedentop notes the role played by Bishops with individualising Christian be-

Following subsequent attempts by emperors and monarchs to co-opt this model of divine right sovereignty, the issue of biblical interpretation came to the fore. In chapter 3, we saw that the Protestant reformers had monarchical patrons and protectors, and the question that arises at this point is: how aware were these monarchs of the implications of their charges' positions? What is at stake here is the extent to which the developments brought about by this patronage resulted from careful theological debate, and the extent to which they resulted from narrow and particular concerns over the issue of governance. Can it reasonably be argued that Richard II and Frederick III were significantly concerned with the theological and anthropological issues raised by the rejection of the Catholic Church's authority? Furthermore, can it even be argued that the theologians themselves understood the full implications of their positions? While many of the rulers and their theological allies do seem to have been devout and sincere, it strains credibility to ascribe to them an appreciation of the ramifications of their claims. The Protestant reformers were attempting to turn the Church back to a primitive state, not to provide the basis for modern empiricism or human rights.

The history of consensual theories of government, culminating in popular sovereignty, demonstrates very well the power driven and irrational nature of the development of these theological accounts. In those areas where it developed, there is scant evidence that the theoretical implications were understood beyond whether it supported a specific claim to a throne, or denied legitimacy to a competitor. So it was in France which, during the 16th century, proved a fertile ground for various theories of legitimacy as a result of the various dynastic disputes between the House of Guise (nominally Catholic), the House of Bourbon (nominally Huguenot Protestant), and whoever was in the position of monarchical authority, such as Catherine de Medici who seems to have played both factions against each other with little concern over theolo-

---

liefs in the development of the Forum Judicum, the Visigoth legal code, which represented a major shift away from earlier law. In this law, "a stronger commitment to equality emerges. What the clergy introduced into the Visigothic code—although not without ambiguities and vestiges of the past—was the principle that all men have 'equal value in the eyes of the law'." Siedentop, *Inventing the Individual*, 138–9.

gy.[6] At times, Catherine favoured the Huguenots in an effort to reduce the influence of the Guise faction in court, at other times, she favoured the Guise and persecuted the Huguenots when the latter represented a threat. The issue of tolerance and the implications of Protestant thought seemed to matter little beyond the issue of whether the Protestants were of use to the court. The idea that doctrinal matters were devised first, and then practical matters of conflict were conducted in accordance with these doctrines—as is implied by standard modern accounts of the history of political theory—is derisory and doesn't hold up to scrutiny.[7]

This pattern of individualising theological doctrine following the needs of actors in particular positions of the Jouvenelian dynamic is also evident in England in the 17th century, where the various factions disputing authority were not competing houses, but different institutions. Here, it was the dispute between the monarchy and an intransigent Parliament that formed the battleground in question, and we can see that the relevant doctrines to which each faction had recourse at particular times reflected their particular needs and position within the Jouvenelian model. It was the parliamentarians' need to counter the centralisation attempted by the English monarchy that drove them to fashion arguments rejecting it, and the argument they hit upon was, naturally, based on the elevation of the people. The nature of this rejection took both legal and theological forms, with both following this same overall pattern. Such positions would eventually require complementary anthropology, and this was supplied by the likes of John Locke and Thomas Hobbes. It is not a coincidence that

6 As William T. Cavanaugh writes, "Catherine proposed bringing Calvinist and Catholic together under a State-controlled Church modeled on Elizabeth's Church of England. Catherine had no particular theological scruples and was therefore stunned to find that both Catholic and Calvinist ecclesiologies prevented such an arrangement. Eventually Catherine decided that statecraft was more satisfying than theology, and, convinced that the Huguenot nobility were gaining too much influence over the king, she unleashed the infamous 1572 St. Bartholomew's Day massacre of thousands of Protestants." William Cavanaugh, "A Fire Strong Enough to Consume the House: The Wars of Religion and the Rise of the State," *Modern Theology* 11, Issue 4, (October 1995): 401, https://doi. org/10.1111/j.1468-0025.1995.tb00073.x.

7 For a criticism of the mythology surrounding the so-called "Wars of Religion," see William T. Cavanaugh, "The Creation Myth of the Wars of Religion," in *The Myth of Religious Violence*, 123–80.

both Hobbes and Locke were very keen to present a consideration of man that begins from a position of inherent individuality—their political schemes demand it.[8]

If this pattern of political conflict preceding and driving the development of this individualistic anthropology holds for the past, then what of the modern period that followed it? We live in an era of ever greater levels of individualisation, where developments are such as to constitute appeals to group identities (as seen in identity politics, which still represents groups of individuals); the underlying principle remains the same, in that they are all primarily directed at intermediary institutions, and, by default, call for the expansion of centralised Power. Internal coherency, and coherency vis-à-vis other parallel cultural developments, is of little concern beyond this function as an assistant to centralising Power. At this point, the idea presents itself that in any situation where we see the success of individualising or equalising accounts of society, we will also see the fingerprints of conflict between various centres of power. A pertinent example of this is the phenomenon of rights which in the modern period increase in number and scope seemingly on a daily basis, and all of which are placed under the umbrella term of "human rights." If we can find conflicts behind these rights, and if we can locate a centre of power expanding its power under the banner of such rights, then this will provide significant support to our model. Unsurprisingly, we do indeed find all of these elements when we review the history of human rights in general.

Human rights have gone through roughly three general developments. The first development was the 18th century application thereof, in which these rights were put forth as self-evident, as seen in the Declaration of Independence:

> We hold these truths to be self-evident, that all men are created equal, that they are endowed by their Creator with certain unalienable Rights, that among these are Life, Liberty and the pursuit of Happiness.

---

8   Consider Hobbes' famous passage in *De Cive*, chapter VII, "Let us return again to the state of nature, and consider men as if but even now sprung out of the earth, and suddainly *(like* Mushromes) come to full maturity without all kind of engagement to each other" Thomas Hobbes, *De Cive: The English Version* (Clarendon Press: Oxford, 1983), 117.

These "self-evident" rights were used as a means to undermine monarchical authority and, in the case of the United States of America, states' rights in the name of the people.[9]

The second development of note can be seen with the United Nations' *Universal Declaration of Human Rights*. This document was drawn up for the UN in the wake of WWII by a transnational elite with clear aspirations to world governance. That it should appeal to all of humanity, and should deign to grant to all equality as well as a newly minted collective identity, seems very much like a repetition of James Madison's invention of the American "people." In this case, it is not the sovereignty of individual continental states being targeted, but rather that of nation-states.

Finally, a much less recognised development of human rights occurred in the early 1970s. This last development is of special importance as it is not widely known beyond specialised histories of human rights, and only clearly comes to light upon recognising the connection between conflict and the expansion of individualising culture. A review of Google's Ngram for the term "human rights" provides us with our first clue as to this development, and it shows that a significant increase in the use of the term occurred following 1973 (Fig. 1). In line with the Jouvenelian model, we should be able to point to a Jouvenelian conflict at this time and the adoption of this term by a set of institutions as a means to undermine other centres of power.

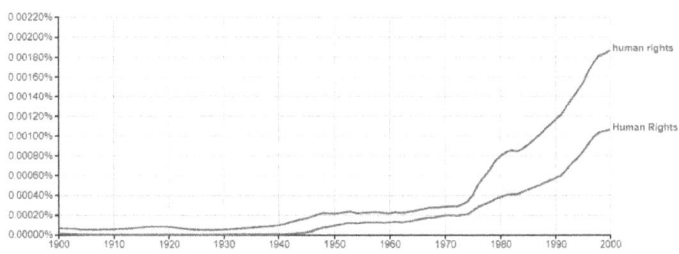

Figure 1. Frequency of the term *human rights* found in Google's text corpora.

At this time, elites in the UN, and specific elements of the Amer-

9   On the shifting basis provided for human rights through history, see Alasdair MacIntyre, *After Virtue: A Study in Moral Theory* (Notre Dame: University of Notre Dame Press, 2007), 69–70.

ican power structure, began to focus on the concept of human rights as a means to undermine the legitimacy of Latin dictatorships, communist regimes, and, most importantly, the foreign policies of the Republican presidency of Richard Nixon. This final point of conflict is central, and well within the Jouvenelian dynamic of rival centres engaging in conflict over political centralisation. Human rights were not first devised and then implemented; they were raised to prominence by the needs of particular actors in the midst of conflict. As Clair Apodaca writes of structural conflict's importance to the adoption of human rights in 1970s American foreign policy in *Understanding U.S. Human Rights Policy: A Paradoxical Legacy*:

> U.S. human rights policy was not an intentionally planned strategy. Congress saddled presidential foreign and domestic policy initiatives with human rights mandates in order to restrain the immoral, if not illegal, behavior of an imperial president.[10]

To this end, Congress, dominated by the Democrat Party, voted to withhold funds for foreign assistance programs—something which had never been done before—and began congressional hearings in the Subcommittee on International Organizations. These hearings, led by Democratic Party congressman Donald Fraser, were justified on the basis of concerns over "rampant violations of human rights and the need for a more effective response from both the United States and the world community."[11] The result of these hearings was a report entitled *Human Rights in the World Community: A Call for U.S. Leadership*,[12] which led to the State Department creating the Office of Coordinator for Humanitarian Affairs.[13] This report also called for greater promotion

10 Clair Apodaca, *Understanding U.S. Human Rights Policy: A Paradoxical Legacy* (New York: Taylor & Francis, 2013), 29.

11 ibid., 33.

12 U.S. House of Representatives, report of the Subcommittee on International Organizations and Movements of the Committee on Foreign Affairs, *Human Rights in the World Community: A Call for U.S. Leadership*, 93rd Congress, 2nd Session, 1974. Washington: GPO, 1974.

13 Apodaca, *Understanding U.S. Human Rights Policy*, 33. Also see Lars Schoultz, *Human Rights and the United States Policy Towards Latin America* (Princeton: Princeton University Press, 1981), 123–24.

of the concept of human rights in the UN and beyond, something which was evidently achieved.[14]

This complicated institutional conflict created a rather odd situation wherein elements of the US governmental structure were engaged in serious conflict with each other, while at the same time engaging foreign actors in two distinct ways. The presidency, under the influence of Henry Kissinger, enacted fairly standard state-to-state diplomacy on the basis of a worldview which saw foreign affairs as the preserve of sovereign states, while Congress, the State Department, and actors in the UN, engaged in a subversive appeal to an international human individual.[15] Among this second group, a further set of institutions comes to light when we apply the Jouvenelian model: the non-governmental foundations, with the Ford Foundation being especially notable. These foundations formed a formidable source of revenue, by which elites connected with this Democratic Party faction could institutionalise human rights independent of governmental channels. These foundations, being "private," were free to dispose of their significant funds without taxation, and were used extensively as tools of foreign policy by specific elements of this elite. The adoption of human rights by the Ford Foundation proves instructive in how these institutions were linked.

In 1975, a report was created by David Heaps, nominally in response to the military dictatorships in South America. This was presented to the Ford Foundation trustees in 1975, following the Pinochet coup, with the title *Human Rights and Intellectual Freedom*.[16] Following the acceptance of Heaps' recommendations that human rights be adopted as a major concern, the Ford Foundation began to devote significant resources to human rights or-

14 The wording of this document is very interesting in that human rights, as applied to all nations, is directly and expressly linked with the rights outlined in the US Constitution on page nine. Here it is written, "Respect for human rights is fundamental to our own national tradition. It is expressed unequivocally in our Constitution."

15 For a summary of the various approaches to foreign policy and their relationship to the concept of human rights, see Apodaca, *Understanding U.S. Human Rights Policy*.

16 The events surrounding this episode are found in detail in William Korey, *Taking on the World's Repressive Regimes: The Ford Foundation's International Human man Rights Policies and Practices* (New York: Palgrave Macmillan, 2007).

ganisations, and even began to create its own.[17] Korey notes the connection here to the congressional hearings held by Donald Fraser, and also makes the same connection as Apodaca does between the hearings and the Nixon administration, even if he does display credulity as to the coincidental nature of both the Ford Foundation and Congress concentrating on human rights at the same time:

> by a striking coincidence, human rights emerged as a critical concern during precisely those years in the U.S. Congress, specifically in the House of Representatives [ ] Its Subcommittee on International Organizations and Movements, headed by Congressman Donald M. Fraser (a Democrat from Minnesota), held unprecedented hearings on U.S. human rights policy [...] As some of the most important congressmen sat on the subcommittee and its parent body, the report was certain to attract attention. Notably unusual was the phrase in its title, "Call for U.S. Leadership." It reflected an angry rejection of the Nixon administration policy, of which Secretary of State Henry A. Kissinger was a principal architect, and a demand for a radically new orientation in American policy.[18]

These human rights organisations, funded by the Ford Foundation in conjunction with other influential foundations,[19] were then put to use in undermining not only the Latin dictatorships, but also, towards the end of the 1970s, the communist regimes of Eastern Europe by way of the Helsinki accord.[20] Soviet acceptance of the presence of human rights watch groups with this accord would

17 The centrality of the Ford Foundation to the development of the Human Rights Watch organisation in particular is covered in detail by Korey. The synthetic nature of this organisation and the determination of its goals by the management of the Ford Foundation, especially by McGeorge Bundy, comes across very clearly from Korey's research. Korey, *Taking on the World's Repressive Regimes.*
18 ibid., 70.
19 Among the other more prevalent foundations were George Soros' Open Society Foundations which were aggressively active across Eastern Europe. Paulina Pospieszna, *Democracy Assistance from the Third Wave: Polish Engagement in Belarus and Ukraine* (Pittsburgh: University of Pittsburgh Press, 2014), 77–78.
20 Korey is, again, exceptionally informative on this matter, noting that Principal VII and Basket 3 of the Helsinki Accords provided, in the words of Yuri Orlov, "an invaluable lever...to the democrats." Korey, *Taking on the World's Repressive Regimes*, 90.

prove to be a disastrous mistake, one which effectively allowed subversive American institutions to develop and operate within Soviet territories. It would be naive to believe that the elites in these different institutions (Congress, the foundations, the UN) were not coordinating informally.

From a modern political perspective, it is possible to model the collapse of the Soviet Union as being somehow a spontaneous event led by mass uprisings, or to turn to the old canard that the Soviets bankrupted themselves with the Afghan War, but from a Jouvenelian angle there is a strong argument to be made that this foundation funding and the institutions it supported provided the institutional structure for the revolutions that brought down communist governments. This argument is supported by the fact that the movements that led to the replacement governments, and a vast number of the members of these new governments themselves, were heavily connected to these foundations and organised human rights groups. The examples of the Solidarity organisation and Lech Walesa in Poland, as well as Charter 77 which was key to the Velvet Revolution in the Czech Republic, are just two of many.[21]

The almost total blindness in standard historical accounts to the role of foundation money and expertise results from a number of blind spots imposed by the liberal view of political structures. We will revisit this in depth in later chapters, but for now, it suffices to quote Korey on the obvious confusion of Henry Kissinger over the significance of human rights funding in undermining the Soviet governments in Eastern Europe:

> Kissinger now acknowledged that Basket 3 (which he earlier had never even noticed in his writing) turned out to be "most significant" and "was destined to play a major role in the disintegration of the Soviet satellite orbit." He went on to add the startlingly unbecoming comment that Basket 3 "became a testimonial to all human rights activists in NATO countries." It was these human rights activists, he suddenly recognized, "who deserve tribute," for it was "the pressures which they exerted" that hastened the end of totalitarian rule. Especially accorded praise were the "heroic reformers in Eastern Europe"—the NGOs of Poland, Czechoslovakia,

---

21 Korey, *Taking on the World's Repressive Regimes*, 91–92.

and Hungary—who used Basket 3 as "a rallying point" in their struggle against "Soviet domination."[22]

These NGOs were clearly those funded by the foundations, and without this funding, it is hard to imagine how these NGOs could have operated, and without these NGOs, it is hard to see how the revolutions could have succeeded.

It is notable here that these actions by this section of the American elite are, in many ways, clearly of a Jouvenelian character. Congress, ceasing merely to represent the American people, took upon itself the task of representing the supposedly suffering people of the entire world as a justification for curtailing the actions of the executive. In addition, abstract rights, somehow held irrespective of the social setting and political order, are invoked and set against a presidency seen as overweening, just as they were cited against the kings by parliamentarians. At this point, these rights, unlike the rights of the American Constitution, have no grounding in natural law, nor do they claim to be derived from God; according to the UN Universal Declaration of Human Rights, they just exist. Aryeh Neier, in *The International Human Rights Movement*, notes this characteristic of the UN Declaration, and attempts to explain its adoption as a means to an end, this end being the furthering of the "cause of peace."[23] He thereby gives it an ethical basis as an element of a consequentialist system which has "peace" as its teleological goal. This is a rather remarkable admission of the intellectual vacuity of human rights from a very influential and important proponent. In Neier's favour, he clearly understands that appeals to human rights are implicitly appeals to laws higher than positive law, but the reader is left at a loss as to what these laws are, as he does not explain. How can he when the authors of the Universal Declaration of Human Rights, the "lodestar"[24] of human rights, do not? This is why his chapter "What are Rights?" does not actually answer the question beyond stating that:

Among those engaged in the promotion of human rights,

22 Korey, *Taking on the World's Repressive Regimes,* 115–16.
23 Aryeh Neier, *The International Human Rights Movement: A History* (Princeton: Princeton University Press, 2012), 96.
24 ibid., 59.

there is general agreement that rights are an aspect of humanity. They are not dependent on such characteristics as race, nationality, or gender, nor do they depend on a person's presence within the territory of a particular political entity.[25]

So, we can see again that, on the one hand, he views human rights as predicated on natural law, but on the other hand, he cannot make this explicit because it is not explicit in the UN's formulation. So clearly, the development of human rights, in response to political stimuli, predates the intellectual justification for such rights, which is still in the process of *creation* at this very moment.[26]

The various developments of rights that we have charted up until the present now appear to have a systematic nature, even if proponents do not fully appreciate it. By developing human rights or the individual as concepts, the thinkers of modernity have been providing intellectual justifications for a specific structure of authority. That there were, and are, advocates who have not understood themselves as doing so is irrelevant to the result. Indeed, we could argue that the less aware the thinkers are of this relationship between the individual and a centralised structure, the more earnest and effective the intellectual disguise for it will be. Disturbingly, this charge can be levelled not only at the theorists of human rights and the individual, but can be levelled across vast areas of modern thought. There is scarcely any aspect of modern thought which does not, in some way, depend on, or imply, the individual that has followed in the wake of political conflicts. In the next chapter, we will consider the implications this has for our understanding of the development of epistemology and ethics, and the further conclusions to be drawn from the relationship between thought and the structures of authority.

---

25 Neier, *The International Human Rights Movement*, 57.
26 There are many examples in Neier's book where he candidly recognises the political conflict-linked nature of rights. For example, he writes, "Twentieth-century assertions that economic and social rights deserved the same degree of recognition and protection as civil and political rights was in part a reaction to the rise of communism and socialism in the nineteenth century. In like manner, twentieth century endorsement of a right of self-determination derives from the rise of another ideology during the nineteenth century: nationalism." Neier, *The International Human Rights Movement*, 64.

V

TRADITIONS AND PATRONAGE

In light of the Jouvenelian model, we see that the new ways of life ushered in by the advent of modern, centralised structures of authority presented those living under this new arrangement with a world for which their immediate conceptual stocks and traditions were ill-suited. This is not to say that these inherited concepts were in any way wrong; it is, rather, to say that an order which has produced a centralised political structure, and whose inhabitants increasingly come to understand themselves as owing political allegiance solely to this centralised political structure, will need new intellectual resources that reflect this understanding. Unfortunately, during this transition, a recognition of the contingency of these new ideas has been lost. To support this claim, we shall present an account of the history of modern philosophy that connects specific developments to patterns of existence within the framework of Jouvenel's model. At this point, we are fortunate enough to be able to call upon the assistance of Alaisdair MacIntyre's epistemological and ethical criticisms of modernity which, in many ways, accord with the model outlined by Jouvenel.

Central to MacIntyre's many criticisms of modern philosophy is his conception of a tradition. For MacIntyre, one major error promulgated by the thinkers of the Enlightenment was that they believed that they could begin from a position of radical doubt, one which rejected the premise that thought was necessarily dependent on time, place, language, and tradition. A tradition, in the MacIntyrean sense, is understood as:

> ...an argument extended through *time* in which certain fundamental agreements are defined and redefined in terms of two kinds of conflict: those with critics and enemies external to the tradition who reject all or at least key parts of those fundamental agreements, and those internal, interpretative debates through which the meaning and rationale of the fundamental agreements come to be expressed and by whose progress a tradition is constituted.[1]

As to the origin of this modern philosophical project, at least in the realm of ethics, MacIntyre is clear that it derives from the shared northwestern Protestant and Jansenist Catholic European culture from which these thinkers came, the precepts of which they attempted to universalise and decontextualise.[2] Where we shall diverge from MacIntyre is in adding the influence of structures of authority with reference to the Jouvenelian structural model; in so doing, we will provide explanations for some of the philosophical developments which he traces in ethics and epistemology, but for which he does not offer a plausible mechanism. Doing so will require us to outline the overall Jouvenelian context within which these attempts at formulating non-tradition-based forms of thought developed. It will also require us to extend MacIntyre's complaint that the thinkers of modernity have blinded us to "a conception of rational enquiry as embodied in a tradition"[3] with the additional claim that, in so doing, they have also blinded us to the role of power centres in selecting and shaping these traditions.

It is with the arrival of first principles of a foundationalist nature that modern philosophy is inaugurated. A first principle of the modern kind, as noted by MacIntyre in *First Principles, Final Ends, and Contemporary Philosophical Issues*,[4] was supposed to fulfil

---

1 Alasdair MacIntyre, *Whose Justice? Which Rationality?* (Notre Dame: University of Notre Dame Press, 1988), 12.
2 See MacIntyre, "Why the Enlightenment Project of Justifying Morality Had to Fail," in *After Virtue*, 51–61.
3 MacIntyre, *Whose Justice?*, 7.
4 Alasdair MacIntyre, *First Principles, Final Ends, and Contemporary Philosophical Issues* (Milwaukee: Marquette University, 1990).

two functions:

> It had to warrant an immediate justified certitude on the part of any rational person who uttered it in the appropriate way, perhaps in the appropriate circumstances. It belongs, that is, to the same class of statements as "I am in pain," "This is red here now" and "I am now thinking." But, on the other hand, it had, either by itself or as a member of a set of such statements, to provide an ultimate warrant for all our claims to knowledge.[5]

The paradigmatic example of such a project is that of René Descartes and his *cogito ergo sum*. In epistemological schemes of this kind, there is a presupposition that epistemology is an internal practice, and can be carried out independent of context.

This pattern of the individual shorn of context forming the basis of philosophical thought is continued in the field of ethics where contemporary philosophers take their cue from their Enlightenment predecessors, and assume that the issue is one of deciphering what the individual must do.[6] This has resulted in the development of two broad branches of ethics in the modern period. The first branch, best represented by Immanuel Kant's categorical imperative, proposes a deontological setting for ethics within which an individual's acts are justified only in so far as they could be willed as a universal law to be followed by all. The second branch, consequentialism, is best represented by the tradition of utilitarianism, as formulated by Jeremy Bentham. Within this scheme, the ethical status of an act is predicated on the aggregated level of happiness that it produces. The central logic of this system is that happiness provides a teleological standard according to which the act can be measured, so that something is good if it conduces to greater happiness, and bad if it conduces to the opposite.[7] So as we can see, in both epistemology and ethics there is a specific pattern of existence implied from the very outset, one which, from the angle of the Jouvenelian model, is

5 MacIntyre, *First Principles*, 11.
6 One of the more famous modern examples is John Rawls' famed veil of ignorance which, by its very nature, precludes anything but the modern individual shorn of context as the basis of ethical thought.
7 See MacIntyre, "Some Consequences of the Failure of the Enlightenment Project," in *After Virtue*, 62–78.

intimately connected to structures of authority. There is an individual; this individual can be considered apart from context; and the structures within which the individual resides are secondary to his individuality.

If we return to the issue of epistemology, and in particular, to the example of René Descartes, we will find that he proves helpful in bridging the gap between the Jouvenelian model and the tradition-based criticism of MacIntyre. This can be accomplished by paying close attention to the connection between the epistemology of Descartes and the patterns of authority within which he thought. From biographical information, we know that Descartes spent his adult life moving between France, Holland, Central Europe, and Germany where he fought in the Thirty Years' War, finally ending his days in Sweden at the court of Queen Christina. The regions wherein Descartes lived, the reader may note, were among those that had been heavily marked by the expansion of Protestant bodies of thought, and by the centralisation that brought them into prominence. While Descartes was, admittedly, a Catholic, this makes little difference, since much of the thought of his time and place, even in Catholic regions, was following the same pattern as Protestant thought, as evidenced by Jansenism. The overall structures of authority made this all but inevitable.[8] We can see the impact of this environment on Descartes, and the influence on him of unacknowledged traditions of thought, when, in the very few times that he was led to write of political matters, he made it clear that he considered philosophical thought to be independent of authority. Given his epistemological approach, this may seem like a strikingly obvious point, but the importance of this position must be brought to the reader's attention because it is dependent on these newly created, centralised structures of authority. That Descartes took this modern structure for granted is also demonstrated in his private correspondence where questions as to his lack of concern with political and moral issues were met with the rejoinder that "only sovereigns, or those authorised by them, have the right to concern themselves with regulating the morals of other people."[9] As we saw in chapter 3, the develop-

---

8 Jansenists, despite being Catholics, adhered to many doctrines shared by Calvinists, such as predestination and justification by faith.
9 Quentin Taylor, "Descartes's Paradoxical Politics," *Humanitas*, Vol. 14, No.2

ment of sovereignty was specific to the geographical area in which Descartes lived; it is not a timeless and neutral position, and this raises obvious questions as to Descartes' Catholicism which, as with Jansenism, was obviously highly adapted to this concept of sovereignty and the supremacy of secular authorities in matters of morals.

This unrecognised context-dependent nature of Descartes' beliefs can also be seen in a letter he wrote to Princess Elizabeth of Bohemia on the topic of Machiavelli's *The Prince*.[10] The details of Descartes' specific agreements or disagreements with Machiavelli's conclusions are of far less importance than his interpretation of Machiavelli's work as a justifiable point of departure for a discussion on the nature of authority. There was clearly a new environment of authority shared between thinkers such as Machiavelli and Descartes, and in sharing this environment, they were driven to articulate new philosophical tools that seemed plausible to themselves, and to those to whom they addressed their writing. This is the world of modern sovereignty and the individual, both present in the work of Machiavelli along with the absence of the idea of a united Christendom with collective standards of behaviour regulating figures of authority.[11] This individual, which both Machiavelli and Descartes recognised, and upon which they based their thought, is a category which, as we have seen, came into being as a result of the centralisation of authority. The creation of this individual is clearly a by-product of Jouvenelian centralisation, but, again, this is not something that we find acknowledged by Descartes, nor by his contemporaries. In positing the individual of modernity, a concept brought into being by political conflict, as the basis for philosophy, Descartes managed, in a profound way, to remove from view the very contingency of this state of affairs. The structures of modernity, and the categories produced in its wake, now become the very basis of reality in the

(Fall 2001): 80, http://www.nhinet.org/taylor14-2.pdf.

10   See the section titled "On Machiavelli's Prince" in Taylor, "Descartes's Paradoxical Politics," 94–102.

11   As MacIntyre notes in *A Short History of Ethics*, "'the individual' appears as starkly in Machiavelli as in Luther. He appears thus because society is not only the arena in which he acts but also a potential raw material, to be reshaped for the individual's own ends, law-governed but malleable." MacIntyre, *A Short History of Ethics*, 128.

form of the thinking individual in Cartesian rationalism.[12] "If we accept that this individual is a product of the Jouvenelian dynamic then, by this act, philosophy in its modern form assumes, and thus by default demands, a political order of centralisation.

In conjunction with the development of this tradition of Cartesian-inspired rationalism, we find a further variant of this individual-centred epistemological pattern being developed in the form of British empiricism. In this case, adherents such as John Locke were overtly concerned with political matters, but this does not make their approach any more self-aware. Just as with Descartes, thinkers in this tradition took the individual of modernity as the basis of their thought, and cast the political structure of centralisation into the background in equal measure, thereby rendering their thought equally powerful in disguising the modern centralisation of authority as simply the grounds of reality. The difference between these two traditions—one favouring individual reasoning as the basis of epistemology (rationalism), the other sensory input (empiricism)—is far less relevant than their point of agreement on the status of this individual as the unquestioned basis of epistemology. Consider the circumstances in which the founders of classical empiricism—Francis Bacon and John Locke—developed their ideas. Bacon, an Anglican, and hardly an apolitical figure, was closely associated with Queen Elizabeth I's court, and then subsequently with King James I's court—with both monarchs in the process of forming centralised political structures of which Bacon was a proponent.[13] This centralised monarchical Power, increasingly overseeing a society of individuals, is furnished with its epistemological underpinning by Bacon in the form of his inductive scientific method which eschews the role of tradition in epistemology. One can even see this societal pattern reflected in works of Bacon other than the *Novum Organum*, including his famous *New Atlantis*, his utopian vision of a centralised structure. The connection between this

---

12 Obviously, this is a point on which modern political theorists such as anarchists would raise issue, given that they believe that the individual can exist separate from any political order. However, from the angle of Jouvenel, we have no indication that such a state of affairs is possible.

13 It is suggestive that Descartes was a great admirer of Bacon, and that he even wrote anonymous positive reviews of his work. See Taylor, "Descartes's Paradoxical Politics," 85.

political order of a centralising Power and the development of individual-derived epistemology is quite evident.[14] In the case of Bacon, one can also see an added influence in his position as attorney-general. Bacon was a functionary of a state apparatus which developed new means of investigating legal cases as part of its expansion into society in general, and, as noted very astutely by Michel Foucault:

> It is perhaps true to say that, in Greece, mathematics were born from techniques of measurement; the sciences of nature, in any case, were born, to some extent, at the end of the Middle Ages, from the practices of investigation.[15]

At every stage, we can see the overwhelming influence of the new political structure within which Bacon operated, and of the traditions which it embodied. In the case of John Locke, the connections between political developments and the social structures devised by these centralising Powers, as well as his epistemology premised on the same Protestant tradition as Bacon, are just as obvious. The philosophical positions demanded by Locke's social contract political theory, a theory developed to rebut the patriarchal natural law claims of Filmer, are supplied by the empiricism that he helped to develop. For this theoretical scheme, Locke needed an individual of a certain kind. This is the pre-social individual of modernity who is capable of contracting into a political order from a state of nature, and whose individuality is, therefore, not dependent on this political order. Any epistemological position which was not, in the first instance, based on a spontaneously arising individuality simply would not do for this political theory, since it would call into question the entire premise that authority was consensual. As with Machiavelli and Luther, Locke's need to reject any dependency of the individual's identity on political

14   The interconnection between epistemology and power is something the French philosopher Michel Foucault recognised when he wrote: "[P]ower produces knowledge (and not simply by encouraging it because it serves power or by applying it because it is useful); that power and knowledge directly imply one another; that there is no power relation without the correlative constitution of a field of knowledge, nor any knowledge that does not presuppose and constitute at the same time power relations." Michel Foucault, *Discipline and Punish: The Birth of the Prison*, trans. Alan Sheridan (New York: Vintage Books, 1995), 27.
15   ibid., 226.

structures which are, in effect, external and secondary to him extends to the issue of property ownership, which led to his famous labour theory of property.[16] Even—or, given the Whig order he was trying to defend, perhaps we should say *unsurprisingly*—in this realm, Locke developed a conception which is conspicuous in placing the acquisition of property prior to, and separate from, authority.

This pre-social individual, so closely connected to the expansive centralising Powers of modernity, not only finds itself established as the basis of modern epistemology, but also becomes the basis of modern ethics; to see how this happened, we can, again, return to the work of Alaisdair MacIntyre.

In MacIntyre's account, the modern development of ethics has been marked by a great number of errors stemming from a failure of ethical accounts to understand the particular settings within which concepts such as "good" or "bad" exist. Whilst these words have persisted, their underlying meaning has repeatedly changed depending on the overall tradition within which they were set. This continuity of words, accompanied by a discontinuity in the underlying schemes or traditions, has produced significant ethical confusion, culminating in the modern period with the development of emotivist accounts of ethics, wherein it is claimed that ethical propositions amount to nothing more than assertions based on emotions.[17] Applying a process of historical analysis to trace the development of these underlying traditions, and thus, to reconstruct the particular settings and schemes within which those earlier thinkers would have understood their ethical claims, has led MacIntyre to conclude that the field of ethics has been subject to three significant systemic changes that have brought us to this emotivism.

In the first instance, ethics in the medieval tradition consisted of an Aristotlean system combined with theistic claims, creating a tradition in which there was:

> …a threefold scheme in which human-nature-as-it-hap-

16 For Locke's theory of property, see John Locke, "Of Property," in *Two Treatises of Government and A Letter Concerning Toleration* (New Haven: Yale University Press, 2003), 111–21.

17 Jouvenel also notes that ethical claims have now become nothing more than a "matter of opinion." Jouvenel, *On Power*, 306.

pens-to-be (human nature in its untutored state) is initially discrepant and discordant with the precepts of ethics and needs to be transformed by the instruction of practical reason and experience into human-nature-as-it-could-be-if-it-realized-its-*telos*. Each of the three elements of the scheme—the conception of untutored human nature, the conception of the precepts of rational ethics and the conception of human-nature-as-it-could-be-if-it-realized-its-*telos*—requires reference to the other two if its status and function are to be intelligible.[18]

In this sense, terms such as "good" and "bad" were evaluative terms, given meaning by the presence of a functional category, and by an overall teleological category against which this functional category is measured. Using the example of evaluating the functionality of a watch, MacIntyre points out that if it can be accepted that a watch is a functional category, and if there is a general agreement as to what a watch should do (i.e. it should tell the time and be portable), a watch can be judged either good or bad by how functional it is.[19] In earlier ethical accounts which found their home within orders wherein the person's position and relation to others were well defined and subject to accepted evaluative criteria, the possibility of applying evaluative judgements did not presuppose a personal preference; it was possible to make evaluative ethical claims which did not devolve into emotivism. This scheme varied between different orders, and its augmentation with theological elements added a set of divinely ordained laws, but, ultimately, it was not significantly altered from a structure which would have been recognisable to Aristotle. This three part scheme then undergoes not one, but two stages of degradation. The first stage involves the removal of the role of reason by Protestant thought, which leaves only the divine laws of theology as the sole teleological guide providing the evaluative measure for ethics:

> Reason can supply, so these new theologies assert, *no* genuine comprehension of man's true end; that power of reason was destroyed by the fall of man. 'Si Adam integer stetisset', on Calvin's view, reason might have played the part that Aristotle assigned to it. But now reason is powerless to correct

18   MacIntyre, *After Virtue*, 53.
19   ibid., 57–58.

our passions (it is not unimportant that Hume's views are those of one who was brought up a Calvinist). Nonetheless the contrast between man-as-he-happens-to-be and man-as-he-could-be-if-he-realized-his-*telos* remains and the divine moral law is still a schoolmaster to remove us from the former state to the latter, even if only grace enables us to respond to and obey its precepts.[20]

The second stage then involves the removal of the teleological function of man by virtue of the rejection of Protestant theology:

> [T]he secular rejection of both Protestant and Catholic theology and the scientific and philosophical rejection of Aristotelianism was to eliminate any notion of man-as-he-could-be-if-he-realized-his-*telos*. Since the whole point of ethics—both as a theoretical and a practical discipline—is to enable man to pass from his present state to his true end, the elimination of any notion of essential human nature and with it the abandonment of any notion of a *telos* leaves behind a moral scheme composed of two remaining elements whose relationship becomes quite unclear.[21]

As we have already noted, the two broad approaches to supplying new moral schemes that follow in the wake of this final change revolve around i) presenting a new categorical status for these moral schemes, or ii) locating a new teleology in the form of naturalistic teleology (such as happiness).

From the angle of the Jouvenelian model, these two stages of degradation in this ethical scheme are notable for corresponding to very specific stages in power conflict within the Western world. In the first instance, the success of Protestantism, after which followed the removal of reason, is tied to the success that Protestant thinkers enjoyed under the centralising monarchs of the Reformation period. The second stage in the degradation of ethics, the removal of theological-based teleology in the 17th and 18th century, corresponds to the age of revolutions and the Enlightenment, and, again, follows in the wake of the success that Enlightenment figures enjoyed under Enlightenment monarchs and the parliamentarians of the Republics. It was those Power

20 MacIntyre, *After Virtue*, 53–54.
21 ibid., 54–55.

centres that arose from the revolutions and assumed the mantle of democratic and republican orders of the people which demanded philosophical accounts that elevated the individual to a point of primacy, and that obfuscated the existence of the primary Power. Political conflict led to the adoption by Power actors of particular strains of thought which were sympathetic to their aims, and in the wake of these politically expedient theories came the philosophical confusion of modernity.

From the Jouvenelian model, we are led to the conclusion that these MacIntyrean traditions are inescapably connected to structures of authority, something which Jouvenel hints at on a number of occasions, but does not develop into a comprehensive account of the history of ideas.[22] The closest that Jouvenel comes to developing a position consistent with his model is in his theorising on the manner in which political theories—theories which, in the first instance, are usually conceived as a means to limit the expansion of the primary Power centre of a particular order—have, through time, been demonstrably co-opted by these very same centres, and repurposed in support of their expansion. Jouvenel is able to note this transformation, such as in Rousseau's general will being turned into a justification for totalitarian government, but is unable to account for it in any theoretically sustained way.[23]

If we are to progress further than both Jouvenel and MacIntyre through a synthesis of their insights, we shall have to note that in conjunction with Jouvenel's failure to follow the implications of his thought to theoretical completeness, MacIntyre is unable to account for the developments that he documents. Specifically, MacIntyre is unable to provide a coherent history and mechanism to explain why the ethical and epistemological confusion he traces occurred as it did; however, this should not be understood as a claim that MacIntyre is unaware of this problem, for he is not. In *After Virtue*, he acknowledges this, and makes a distinct call for an account of the connection between traditions and structures of

22 For example, Jouvenel asks, *"Is not the conclusion this: that the great period of rationalism was also that of enlightened and free-thinking despots[?]"* Jouvenel, *On Power*, 211. Jouvenel also points towards this "association of the philosopher with the tyrant" as being systemic. Jouvenel, *On Power*, 132–35.

23 Jouvenel merely describes this tendency as the power centre (Power) possessing "…some mysterious force of attraction by which it can quickly bring to heel even the intellectual systems conceived to hurt it." ibid., 59.

authority throughout history, writing:

> There is a history yet to be written in which the Medici
> princes, Henry VIII and Thomas Cromwell, Frederick the
> Great and Napoleon, Walpole and Wilberforce, Jefferson
> and Robespierre are understood as expressing in their ac-
> tions, often partially and in a variety of different ways, the
> very same conceptual changes which at the level of philo-
> sophical theory are articulated by Machiavelli and Hobbes,
> by Diderot and Condorcet, by Hume and Adam Smith and
> Kant. There ought not to be two histories, one of political
> and moral action and one of political and moral theorizing,
> because there were not two pasts, one populated only by ac-
> tions, the other only by theories. Every action is the bearer
> and expression of more or less theory-laden beliefs and con-
> cepts; every piece of theorizing and every expression of belief
> is a political and moral action.[24]

This work is, in many ways, an attempt to answer this call, and
part of doing so requires alteration to MacIntyre's conception of
traditions. As we saw in MacIntyre's definition of traditions, the
shape and development of traditions is defined as the result of
"fundamental agreements" which "are defined and redefined" in
relation to internal and external debates. This picture is lacking in
that, as can be seen from a Jouvenelian angle, it is observably the
case that the success of a given tradition is often less due to dialectical debate, or to the collective acceptance of the superiority
of a given position, than it is due to brute force and institutional
prevalence, especially when the issue at hand is one immediately touching on matters of power.[25] This criticism, however, does
not undermine the overall accuracy of MacIntyre's account of
traditions; rather, it adds a further mechanism for the determination of success, and emphasises the connection between traditions and structures of authority that is implicit in MacIntyre's
thought throughout *After Virtue*. At many points in *After Virtue*,
he raises criticisms against bureaucracy and bureaucratic individ-

---

24 MacIntyre, *After Virtue*, 61.
25 Take, for example, the success enjoyed by Lysenkoism in Soviet Russia, as
well as the success of gender ideology in the Western world at present. Neither are
traditions of thought which can plausibly be claimed to have come to prominence
as a result of a process of reasoned debate.

ualism, and against the organisations that embody them such as the corporation and government. In doing so, MacIntyre draws a connection between these organisations and the ethical accounts that they support. Specifically, MacIntyre notes that "it is in the cultural climate of this bureaucratic individualism that the emotivist self is naturally at home."[26] This is further augmented by his observation that the permeation of this individualism into "society" results in political debates becoming debates "between an individualism which makes its claims in terms of rights and forms of bureaucratic organization which make their claims in terms of utility."[27] The connection between structures of authority and traditions is, therefore, already acknowledged by MacIntyre, but not systematically explored.[28]

A key aspect of connecting these structures of authority to traditions is the acknowledgement that these centres of power are selecting traditions and determining the direction in which they develop by a process comparable to the act of patronage. These centres of power provide the resources, institutional embodiment, and protection that allow these traditions to flourish—resources being money and other means of support required for the advocates of a tradition to be sustained without having to provide for themselves, and institutional embodiment and protection being the provision of physical places and the permitting of structures of organisation (such as universities, think tanks, NGO status, and so on).

This process of patronage is subtle, and it has a number of characteristics that allow those involved to misunderstand the re-

26 MacIntyre, *After Virtue*, 35.
27 ibid., 71.
28 Take MacIntyre's recognition that "as Marxists organize and move toward power they always do and have become Weberians in substance, even if they remain Marxists in rhetoric; for in our culture we know of no organized movement towards power which is not bureaucratic and managerial in mode and we know of no justifications for authority which are not Weberian in form. And if this is true of Marxism when it is on the road to power, how much more so is it the case when it arrives. All power tends to coopt and absolute power coopts absolutely." MacIntyre, *After Virtue*, 109. This Weberian form being that "on Weber's view no type of authority can appeal to rational criteria to vindicate itself except that type of bureaucratic authority which appeals precisely to its own *effectiveness*. And what this appeal reveals is that bureaucratic authority is nothing other than successful power." ibid., 26.

lationship between authority and traditions. First, there is the rejection of traditions which concomitantly demands an anarchistic ontological account of the spread and development of ideas; in modern conceptions, ideas seem to simply appear and then succeed by popularity or by dint of being evidently correct. Second, there is the separation between the patrons and those receiving patronage; those developing variants of existing traditions are not (usually) doing so in response to instigation from power centres, but in accordance with some genuine belief in a pursuit of truth. Finally, this process is hidden from view by the manner in which these developments can, indeed, be seen to follow the logic inherent within traditions. As we saw in earlier chapters with the path taken by theories of sovereignty and legitimacy, there is an observable series of logical steps from one position to another, and this can quite effectively disguise the role of institutional actors in this process not only from other actors, but also from the thinkers working within a tradition. We can see many of these elements in play with the aforementioned developments in epistemology and ethics where it appears that the thinkers, whether aware of it or not, were, and still are, auditioning for selection and promotion by actors within the power structure who, upon needing their intellectual support, called them forward and brought them into prominence. Again, this should not be mistaken as a claim that these thinkers were in any sense cynical producers of intellectual systems for reward. Unless there is good reason to think otherwise, we should accept that these thinkers were genuinely attempting to further intellectual understanding. Despite this, we must, yet again, agree with MacIntyre that these thinkers, in developing these new ethical systems, "did not recognize their own peculiar historical and cultural situation,"[29] and, we may add, they did not understand that their thoughts and beliefs were shaped by political centralisation and the individualisation of society that followed in its wake.[30]

With the addition of this concept of traditions, Jouvenel's model suggests a regularity created by the limitations occasioned by

---

29   MacIntyre, *After Virtue*, 55.

30   At many points MacIntyre points towards the connection between structures of authority and the systems of thought propagated by them, such as with his criticisms of bureaucratic individualism throughout *After Virtue*.

this tradition-bound nature of thought. The human agent, acting within human orders, must operate from a specific tradition that supplies him with the concepts and language with which he can think and engage with the world. Some proof of this is provided by noting that centres of authority evidently do not select ideas and concepts which differ vastly from the tradition within which they exist, but rather, select variations of existing traditions. The development of theories of divine right sovereignty in chapter 3 gives insight into this process of internal redirection of traditions.

Another point of note that follows from this issue of traditions is that the Jouvenelian model provides strong support for theories of language of a Sapir-Whorf type, a relationship further supported by MacIntyre's theory of tradition. Jouvenel himself was only vaguely aware of this issue, and we can see how this lack of awareness of the linguistic constraints created by traditions in framing and shaping rational thought undermined him in a further example related to the issue of the individual we saw in chapter 4. This is the issue of altruism, which is of great importance, as Jouvenel attempted to model the behaviour of power centres as being driven by altruism.[31] The claim that there is such a thing as altruism would, if presented to those within the Western world, likely prove to be not only uncontroversial, but self-evidently obvious, so much so that scientists in a number of fields take altruism to be a valid, scientifically neutral concept.[32] However, a closer inspection of the concept from a Jouvenelian angle provides grounds to conclude that the concept has been shaped by political conflict, and is dependent on a tradition which has itself been determined by the structure of authority.

Etymologically, the word altruism dates to 1830 and was coined by Auguste Comte as a means to refute egoism.[33] The word and the concept were then introduced into English in an

31 Jouvenel describes Power, as well as all other centres of power, as being driven by "altruistic externals." Jouvenel, *On Power*, 119.
32 For a far fuller account of the impact of concepts such as altruism and their adoption as scientific concepts, see Anna Wierzbicka, "Doing Things with Other People: 'Cooperation,' 'Interaction,' and 'Obśćenie'," in *Imprisoned in English: The Hazards of English as a Default Language* (Oxford: Oxford University Press, 2014), 101–16.
33 Mary Pickering, *Auguste Comte: An Intellectual Biography, Volume Two* (Cambridge: Cambridge University Press, 2009), 7.

1853 translation of Comte's work, and popularised by George H. Lewes,[34] and later, by Herbert Spencer. Noting this historical origin is important, as modern proponents of altruism present it as being, in some sense, timeless, and have even managed to unearth altruism from every religion in the world. If, however, altruism is universal, then we are left with the question as to why it took until Auguste Comte for it to be articulated. The answer implied by liberal modernity is that it must have always existed, and that previous orders and other cultures must simply have been ignorant of the matter.[35] An alternative conclusion is that Comte did not discover a timeless concept, but instead, developed a concept which is itself dependent on a series of prior concepts, and which is only comprehensible within a specific tradition of thought. This tradition is that of liberal modernity and the establishment of thought premised on the individual. Consider that for altruism to develop there first had to be an egoism that would define it and form its binary opposite; and it is with Descartes, Bacon, and Hobbes that we find this egoism in the creation of the individual of modernity which we have seen was a politically determined tradition of thought. It is only when faced with this modern individual—a pre-social, discrete entity—that the problem of understanding sociability arises. At this point, there arises a need to explain why these individuals would act in a way which is not wholly for themselves, and subsequently, the concept of altruism comes to the fore.

With the arrival of Darwin's theory of evolution, this ethical system was provided with a supposedly scientific basis, but the connection between Darwin's theory and the power structure that brought about Comte's thought is even more clear. The clarity of this connection is apparent when we consider that Darwin's

---

34 Mary Pickering, *Auguste Comte: An Intellectual Biography, Volume Three* (Cambridge: Cambridge University Press, 2009), 117.

35 Take, for example, the introductory textbook *Altruism*, which asserts that "It is valued by (almost) everyone and its core meaning universally agreed. Altruism, in its broadest sense, means promoting the interests of the other." There is no recognition that altruism is untranslatable, merely that some value it and others may not, which implies that all recognize it—in other words, it is a universal of humanity. Niall Scott and Jonathan Seglow, *Altruism* (Maidenhead: Open University Press, 2007), 1.

thought finds its origins in political economy,[36] as Jouvenel notes:

> It was survival of the fittest, an idea which, as is known, was not suggested to Darwin by the spectacle of nature, but was, on the contrary, taken by him from the philosophers of individualism.[37]

Darwin's original claims rested on a system within which the survival of discrete individuals in the shape of organisms came first, and whose sociability, like the individual of modern philosophy, therefore, was secondary. It is no wonder that, after the publication of *The Origin of Species*,[38] liberals were exceptionally enthusiastic about Darwin's theory, as he was, in a sense, reflecting their philosophical presumptions back to them under the guise of a science. We even find this connection between Darwinian theories and modern liberal philosophy being made explicit by the likes of Darwin's "bulldog," Thomas Huxley, who wrote of early man that:

> As among these, so among primitive men, the weakest and stupidest went to the wall, while the toughest and shrewdest, those who were best fitted to cope with their circumstances, but not the best in any other sense, survived. Life was a continual free fight, and beyond the limited and temporary relations of the family, the Hobbesian war of each against all was the normal state of existence. The human species, like others, plashed and floundered amid the general stream of evolution, keeping its head above water as it best might, and thinking neither of whence nor whither.[39]

And, even more to the point, he declared of Darwin's work that "every philosophical thinker hails it as a veritable Whitworth gun in the armory of liberalism."[40]

---

36 Jouvenel also notes the connection between political thought and Darwinism in the inheritance of the concept of division of labor by the biological sciences from political thought, but does not treat this with sufficient scepticism. Jouvenel, *On Power*, 53.

37 ibid., 351.

38 Charles Darwin, *On the Origin of Species by Means of Natural Selection*, (New York: Simon & Schuster Paperbacks, 2009).

39 T.H. Huxley, "The Struggle for Existence: A Programme," *Popular Science Monthly*, Vol. 32 (April 1888): 736.

40 T.H. Huxley, review of *The Origin of Species*, by Charles Darwin, *Westminster Review*, Vol. 17, (January 1860): 541–70.

It was within this ecosystem of self-interested individual organisms that Darwin was faced with the supposed problem that Comte was to name. Having basically imported political economy and egoism into the natural world, Darwin faced a problem similar to that faced by modern thinkers: how to explain sociability or behaviour which could not be explained as immediately self-interested, but this time in the realm of biology. Darwin's initial explanation was to posit group-level selection, but this has proven unpopular, and did not survive the development of the neo-Darwinian synthesis of the 20th century.

The celebrated resolution to this problem of eusociality was to mirror the solution resorted to by liberal thinkers, and to conclude that those actions which on the surface appear to be altruistic are actually fully self-serving. This was accomplished with the development of the concept of inclusive fitness which has its political and philosophical partner in the concept of enlightened self-interest. In inclusive fitness, the apparent unselfish behaviour of the individual biological entity in assuming a role which forgoes sexual reproduction, as in the case of ants, or which involves danger, as in the case of species which issue warning calls to others within their group, is explained as actually being selfishness on the genetic level, which is really then selfishness on the individual level after all. The biological entity's sacrifice for those within its group is rewarded by the successful transfer of genetic information shared by the individual with survivors.

Once we accept the contingency of this concept of altruism and its dependency on this liberal tradition, the assertion that it is some universal aspect of humanity, or an aspect of nature, presents itself as yet another instance of modern intellectuals lacking awareness of the effects of power, and of the limitations imposed by traditions and semantic categories on thought, and, in so doing, reinforcing modern structures of authority by enshrining categories which make them unquestionable.

VI

OUR GREEK INHERITANCE

MODERN political thought—the point of orientation for all modern thinkers—has been highly reliant upon political categories deriving from Greek thought. These categories are best summarised by Aristotle's scheme of six political forms. These six categories are subdivided into a further two categories which correspond to their so-called "normal" and "perverted" versions. The normal versions are categorised as monarchy, rule of one; aristocracy, rule of the few; and polity, rule of the many; the respective corrupted forms being tyranny, oligarchy, and democracy. These categories are, therefore, premised on first, the numbers involved in government, and second, the character of those governing. If Power and its position in relation to the rest of an order does, indeed, determine the direction of culture—as would seem to be the case from previous chapters—and, especially, if it determines culture directly relevant to political thought, then in light of this, it would follow that a reassessment of our political categories is in order. Doing so requires us to look closely at the Greek orders whence these political categories arose, to see if the Jouvenelian dynamic of political conflict explains their formulation. Of special interest to us in this reassessment are changes to the category of democracy. Democracy is the only political form currently accepted as legitimate, so it would make a great deal of sense, from a Jouvenelian angle, to presume that this category, in particular, has been favoured by the actions of expansionary Power centres. When we look at the origins of democracy with this hypothesis in mind, we see a series of developments that confirm this hypothesis. It is the Athens of Solon, Peisistratus, and Cleisthenes whence democracy sprang, and this period is marked by a very obvious political centralisation, one with roots in the changes that had been occurring in Greek society for some time before this.[1]

Before democracy entered into human consciousness, the Athenian order, as with all other Greek orders, had a very specific structure which has been documented in great detail in Numa Denis Fustel De Coulanges' *The Ancient City*.[2] These orders, as with other Indo-European orders, were marked by a concentration of authority on the heads of families, the *Eupatrids*, who were concerned with the worship of the family's gods in the form of the family's hearth fire. The maintenance of this fire, and the worship tied to it, could only be continued by the male line, and it was only by preservation of this worship that the needs of the patricians in the afterlife would be met. The result was that this worship was very much contained within the family, and the rites and prayers associated with the worship were passed down orally. At this point, the role of the king was that of high priest, a figure who was simply the head of a confederation of these families with little power to compel the Eupatrids. Over time, this began to change, and by degrees, this central figure of the king began to accumulate power and to set this worship on a city-centred basis rather than a family-centred basis, and the means by which this was achieved was the Jouvenelian dynamic of appeal to the periphery. In this case, the periphery can be found in the form of the clients of the Eupatrids, the *Thetes*. These Thetes, and others who were excluded from the patrician's family worship and did not have a worship of their own, naturally allied with the king, something Coulanges also found repeated in the Italian cities in the time of Rome.

The result of the breakdown of this family-based order was

---

1 That the Greek order was highly centralised is counterintuitive, given our modern celebration of Greek democracy. However, as pointed out by Jouvenel, "the Power in the Greek cities over the citizens was far in excess of that of the Great King over his subjects." Jouvenel, *On Power*, 397.
2 Numa Denis Fustel De Coulanges, *The Ancient City: A Study on the Religion, Laws, and Institutions of Greece and Rome* (Perth: Imperium Press, 2019).

what Coulanges recognised as three revolutions which occurred in succession. The first of these revolutions—the accumulation of power by the kings with the assistance of these peripheral figures—resulted in the government of the city becoming more pronounced. This did not result in the success of royalty as it was ultimately overthrown by the aristocracy throughout the Greek world, but this did not matter as a centralisation of government had occurred regardless. That the aristocracy occupied this government did not alter this fact; the underlying structures of authority had changed. The second revolution occurred due to what Coulanges recognised as a discrepancy between this centralised, city-based government and the previous, family-focused organisation which the aristocracy attempted to maintain. Despite the aristocracy occupying this government, those in this centralised position were subject to the imperative of this position, and became, by degrees, patrons of the lower orders in much the same way as the kings before them had. The result of this revolution was a gradual, but definitive, end to the tradition of primogeniture. By this act, the patrician no longer held the total power he once had. The family authority, based on this primogeniture, or direct inheritance of the eldest son, was broken.

Subsequent to the revolution which brought centralisation, and to that which broke the inheritance pattern and authority structure of the ancient families, there followed a third revolution, this time of the plebeians who had been drawn to the cities. These were men who had no relation to the family's worship in any sense, unlike the clients, or even slaves, who were part of the family structure. They formed, in Coulanges' opinion, a separate society that lived in parallel to that of the aristocracy. With this revolution, we find the rise of the tyrants who allied with this plebeian class to form centralised points of governance dominated by a single individual. It is here that we find democracy's beginnings in the reforms of Solon who was tasked with reducing the tensions created by the increase in the plebeian class.

If we begin with Solon's reforms, and if we agree with standard accounts that they represent a turning point in the advance of what we accept as democracy,[3] we find that these reforms show

3 For a standard narrative of the development of Greek democracy from Solon to Pericles, see Thomas N. Mitchell, *Democracy's Beginning: The Athenian Story*

a great expansion of centralised government intrusion into other elements of the Athenian power structure. Clientship was formally ended, property was separated from the family worship, and the order was marked by a division based on wealth, not on family. This intrusion is so marked that Solon's laws included such matters as the validity of wills, the supply of dowries, and the correct method for the impregnation of brides.[4] There were, supposedly, even details on prices to be set in state-run brothels which Solon had established.[5] None of this would have been possible were it not for the obvious presence of a centralised Athenian government system that could actually enforce these laws. Following the laws of Solon, it is not at all surprising that the groundwork was laid for the so-called "tyranny" of Peisistratus, as this centralised political order was open to occupation by anyone able to grasp and use it, just as Solon had.

At this point, it is interesting to note that approaching these changes from this Jouvenelian angle raises the question of just what the differences were between the so-called "proto-democratic" actions of Solon and the so-called "tyrannical" actions of Peisistratus, since they both utilised the same centralised political pattern to enforce their will. In the reforms of both Solon and Peisistratus, the subsidiary power centres were undermined with appeals to the periphery in the power structure, and the strength of the central government was increased, regardless of the claimed intentions and character of those at the centre. To see this, we can look at the specific actions of Peisistratus. Peisistratus had attempted to gain and hold power in Athens on a number of occasions, and it was only on his third attempt that he managed to both gain and maintain control of the government.[6] Once in power for the final time, Peisistratus implemented a number of changes which would not have been out of place if attributed to

(New Haven: Yale University Press, 2015). Also, see David Stockton, "From Solon to Ephialtes," in *The Classical Athenian Democracy* (New York: Oxford University Press, 1991), 19–56.

4   Alan E. Samuel, "Plutarch's Account of Solon's Reforms," *Greek, Roman, and Byzantine Studies*, Vol. 4, No. 4 (1963): 231–36, https://grbs.library.duke.edu/index.

5   Sarah B. Pomeroy, *Goddesses, Whores, Wives and Slaves: Women in Classical Antiquity* (London: Hale, 1975), 57.

6   See Brian M. Lavelle, *Fame, Money, and Power: The Rise of Peisistratos and "Democratic" Tyranny at Athens* (Ann Arbor: University of Michigan Press, 2005).

Solon. These included the introduction of travelling judges, state loans to citizens in the lower sections of society, and the institution of public cults.[7] The goal of such policies, as indicated by Jouvenel, was to undermine the control of the traditional nobility of Athens, a nobility on whom Peisistratus' power did not rest, and which was hostile to him. The policy of instituting travelling judges has clear parallels in the actions of centralising monarchs in medieval Europe who followed exactly the same path. The reader may recall the example of Henry II's legal reforms referenced in chapter 1, as they are a perfect point of comparison. The goal of such an action is to open up legal recourse to sections of the society that had previously relied on local means of justice, which brings these sections of society into direct contact with the government, furthering popular support for the centralised Power centre, and weakening these intermediaries.

The allowance of state loans can also be explained, according to the Jouvenelian model, as a change that undermined the nobility's power and increased the dependence of the common people on the primary Power of the Athenian government. Such an action alters to whom debt is owed, and debt is intrinsically linked to power, as can been seen when debt relief is recognised as a key and recurring political issue in all pre-modern orders that had a monetary system. We see this very clearly in the actions of Solon: the relief of debt brought about by his currency reforms, and the simple cancellation of debts, were cornerstones of his reforms. The targets of such relief, those who would be weakened, were the lenders, the relatively wealthy landowners—the nobility, yet again.[8] This is another example with clear parallels in the histo-

7 See Carl Hampus Lyttkens, *Economic Analysis of Institutional Change in Ancient Greece: Politics, Taxation and Rational Behaviour* (London: Routledge, 2015) for an account of the actions of many Greek politicians such as Peisistratus, an account which exhibits a striking affinity with the Jouvenelian model. In particular, note that Lyttkens describes Peisistratus' actions as being targeted at disempowering the nobility, and recognises that his loans to farmers and the institution of travelling judges, "reduced the dependence of the common people on the traditional aristocracy." Lyttkens, *Economic Analysis,* 58.

8 There is also a possibility that this class of lenders included foreign elements from Athens' competitor, Aegina, see J.G. Milne, "The Economic Policy of Solon," *Hesperia: The Journal of the American School of Classical Studies at Athens,* Vol. 14, No. 3 (July–September 1945): 234, https://www.jstor.org/stable/146709. Another interpretation is provided by Coulanges who proposes that it is unlikely that there

ry of medieval Europe, especially with regards to Solon's currency reforms. In the medieval period, the issue of control over the
money supply was often a battleground upon which the monarchy and nobility clashed, since currency debasement, or inflation,
benefited the monarchy, borrowers, and those on fixed payment
relationships (normally, the lower classes), whilst, conversely,
maintaining a stable currency supply without debasement and
subsequent inflation benefited the lenders and landholders who
were normally the nobility.[9] The monarchies benefited, as they
could issue currency of lesser quality, and could thus purchase
goods and services with less gold or silver; the borrowers and the
poor in society also benefited, as their debts decreased in value
and they were able to purchase more. The lenders obviously had
an interest in maintaining the opposite state of affairs—a loan or
fixed rent in a given coin denomination reduces in value along
with debasement over time.

Athens did not itself issue coinage at the time of Solon; instead, coinage originally minted in various other cities was in
circulation, so debasement of the type favoured in more modern
times was not an option. The solution that Solon supposedly arrived at was to make official alterations to which coinage could
be used to pay debts. The Aegintean drachma, minted in Aegina,
appears to have been the standard currency in use in Athens leading up to the reforms, but by making the drachma-denominat-
ed debts payable in the newly minted drachmas of Chalcis and
Corinth—drachmas which were of less purity than the Aegintean
drachma, and, therefore, of less value—the value of current debts
reckoned in drachmas was greatly reduced. Thereby, Solon suc-
cessfully managed to manipulate currency exchanges in order to
achieve his goal of debt reduction.[10]

were borrowers and lenders at this point in time, and that later translators have
misinterpreted the state of affairs due to anachronistically applying these categories. Instead, Coulanges claims that "In those debtors of whom Plutarch speaks
we must see the former clients; in their debts, the annual rent which they were to
pay to their former masters; and in the slavery into which they fell if they failed
to pay, the former clientship, to which they were again reduced." Coulanges, *The
Ancient City*, 225.

9   See Spufford, "The Scourge of Debasement," in *Money and its Use in Medieval
Europe*, 289–318.

10   "If an Attic farmer had raised a loan and received the cash in Aeginetan
drachmas, and the bond had not been specifically stated to be for drachmas of

As for the changes in the ceremonies that were celebrated in Athens, Peisistratus famously expanded and increased the importance of the Panathenaea, a ceremony in honour of Athena, the goddess representative of Athens. With this centralisation of a cult centred around the city, the pattern of relations was clearly directed in a very specific way. The importance of family worship was reduced, and the direction of society was refocused towards the primary Power of the Athenian government.[11]

This overall Jouvenelian pattern of undermining of subsidiaries in the Athenian order does not stop with Peisistratus' sons; neither does it stop with those that followed them. It also does not stop when we arrive at the development of democracy. The constancy of structural power imperatives rendered the occupant of the centre of the order largely irrelevant. As a result, we find Cleisthenes, the so-called "father of democracy," acting in a purely Jouvenelian way in his reorganisation of Athenian society so as to bind the citizenry directly to the political rule of the city, which decisively ended the influence of the traditional aristocratic structures of power.[12] From this point on, the question of what constituted an Athenian citizen turned on the recognition of the citizen's status by the Athenian governmental apparatus, and not on claims to family relationships. The older order had been broken by a centralised Power which had taken up the mantle of democracy.

From this history, it seems obvious that democracy was not a rationally discovered concept, but was, instead, a cultural production of centralising Power, just as the actions of Solon, Peisistratus, and Cleisthenes clearly were. These power structures acted as selection mechanisms for concepts that accorded with their

a particular standard, it would presumably have been quite legal for him to pay the interest or repay the principal in Chalcidian or Corinthian drachmas of less weight, just as it was legal for the French nation a few years ago to pay the interest on loans raised in francs before 1914 by means of francs of one-fifth the value of the old on the gold standard." Milne, "The Economic Policy of Solon," 238.

11   "Peisistratos spent on public goods. He adorned the city and fostered public cults. This decreased the power of the old nobility." Lyttkens, *Economic Analysis,* 57.

12   See Martin Ostwald, "Cleisthenes and Legislative Procedure" in *From Popular Sovereignty to the Sovereignty of Law: Law, Society, and Politics in Fifth Century Athens* (Berkeley: University of California Press, 1986), 15–28. Also see Lyttkens, "The Road to Democracy Part One: A Structural Approach," in *Economic Analysis,* 52–69.

centralising actions, and this process reached its logical conclusion with democracy, a state of centralised Power wherein this
primary Power ensured its continuance and security by hiding its
true nature. This appeal to the people, which was key to centralisation, could not be presented as the transference of immediate
government by the nobility to distant government in the form of
the archons and tyrants of Athens; instead, what we find is the
claim that this relationship is one of liberation of the common
people, with the government not advertising its role in this relationship. This power structure—which had been subject to Jouvenelian centralising, and to the promotion of cultural trends that
simultaneously hid the role of this primary Power and successful-
ly presented a narrative of the liberation of the citizens—is the
one wherein we find that the political categories were developed.

Thus far, what we have failed to account for is why these
changes occurred when and where they did. Why is it that the
Athenian order moved far further on the road to political centralisation than any order before it, and did so in such an innovative
way? The answer to this lies in the role that the newly developed
coinage played in the formation of Athenian power structures.
The Athenian order of the political categories is no longer the
gift-giving and redistributive order of the earlier Greeks, wherein
the role of a centre of society is clear and overt in the form of a
king or a local prince presiding over sacrifices. Nor is this a tem-
ple-administered redistributive society of the type we see at this
time in Egypt and the Middle East. The general collapse of Greek
society that followed the fall of the Mycenaean civilisation did
not leave an infrastructure that could enable the cities to adopt
this type of system; instead, we have a decentralised society in the
process of centralisation, and which was subject to the new development of money to varying degrees, but monetised nonetheless.[13] This monetisation opened up new patterns of organisation,

13 "In Greece, however, it was probably precisely the collapse of the earlier structure that led to the development of primitive money. The administrators of the
redistributive palace economy needed to know how much barley the king needed,
and how many sheep; how much or how many of each he would have to provide
to each of the people dependent upon him, whether free or slave; but they did not
have to make the calculation of how much barley was worth a single sheep. [...]
When the palaces had been burned and their far-flung bureaucracy dispersed,
there will have been more need for exchange. The Homeric heroes did indeed have

and new means by which the centres of the orders in question could relate to the rest of the order. It opened up means of undermining subsidiary centres of power which did not exist before.

By introducing its own coinage, or by fostering the use of foreign coinage introduced by others, the primary Power could now forgo traditional forms of interaction with the power structure, and could, instead, hire individuals and develop new institutions based on this new system of coinage. It could bypass those institutions and relationships that previously kept its centralisation in check, a process we saw clearly in medieval and early modern Europe in earlier chapters. There was no longer a need to rely on relationships and obligations for military resources.[14] Money had changed everything, and in this regard, Greek society was a crucible of innovation.[15]

One of the results of this change in relationships is that money disguises the role of Power. Power obviously benefits greatly from money, and there is no incentive for those in power to make it clear that their expansion of a monetary economy is driven by power imperatives, but the connection is undeniable. The effects created by this new web of relations are wide-ranging, because overt, visible intervention of political authority is greatly reduced. Prices can now be widely set by markets, interactions can happen in relatively anonymous ways, and these interactions can be one-off and not dependent on continual relationships; yet, these changes are utterly dependent on centralised Power.

This introduction of monetary relationships had the effect of

to weigh the value of a slave against the value of a tripod; if this seems to us a step toward the concept of money, it is not for that reason a sign of an expanding economy." David M. Schaps, *The Invention of Coinage and the Monetization of Ancient Greece* (Ann Arbor: University of Michigan Press, 2015), 71.

14 "Control over the relatively new phenomenon of money allows the tyrant to dispense with the ancient principles of solidarity through kinship and of reciprocity, for he is able to create his following by paying them. Of course, paying mercenaries involves reciprocity in the broad sense that the mercenaries fight in return for pay." Richard Seaford, "Tragic Tyranny," in *Popular Tyranny: Sovereignty and Its Discontents in Ancient Greece,* ed. Kathryn A. Morgan (Austin: University of Texas Press, 2009), 97.

15 "In another world and time, in the later Middle Ages, the increasing use of money and the increasing power of merchants were important factors in the breakdown of manorial ties, and it will be obvious that they may have performed a similar function in Greece and notably so in Athens." Schaps, *The Invention of Coinage,* 119.

necessitating new ways of accounting for existence. Just as with the Enlightenment connections to centralising Power, we find, at the very advent of philosophy, the connection between philosophy and money, and, therefore, between philosophy and centralising centres of power. It is upon the introduction of coinage that we find the development of philosophy. It is not a coincidence that the birth of philosophy accompanies the development and spread of money. Philosophy's birth, with the pre-Socratics in Miletus, occurred in a city much in advance of Athens in the development of modern money. Only once Athens had developed along this same path do we see the philosophy of Socrates, Plato, and Aristotle.[16]

What should interest us concerning the development of the political categories is that the decisive structural changes that occurred—changes which were unique to Greek civilisation of this period—were not noted as such by the philosophers and political theorists elaborating the categories. What they missed, just as the Enlightenment thinkers did, is the Jouvenelian role of Power in bringing about the society that they were trying to understand. This is not to say that the accounts of the philosophers of this time are without value for an understanding of power structures, as they still capture elements of this Jouvenelian process. For example, we get a glimpse of the Jouvenelian dynamic in the writing of Aristotle who makes the observation in Book III of his *Politics* that:

> ...tyrants have foreign guards, for kings rule in accordance with law and over willing subjects, but tyrants rule over unwilling subjects, owing to which kings take their guards from among the citizens but tyrants have them to guard against the citizens.[17]

A point Coulanges also makes very astutely is that the difference between a tyranny and a monarchy seems to rest on a tyranny being governance by an individual in alliance with the periphery,

---

16   For an extended analysis of the connection between the development of monetary relationships and that of philosophy, see Graeber, "The Axial Age (800 BC-600 AD), Materialism II: Substance," in *Debt: The First 5,000 Years*, 243–50.
17   Aristotle, *Politics*, trans. H. Rackham (Cambridge: Harvard University Press, 1959), 251.

while monarchy is government by an individual in alliance with the intermediaries of an order—a point made clear by the conspicuous absence of any sort of religious underpinning for the concept of a tyrant.[18]

It would seem that we owe these political categories to a lack of awareness of the Jouvenelian mechanism. Given this, we are not surprised to find that Aristotle cannot provide robust definitions of the various political forms, as they, at best, poorly capture the Jouvenelian process. Consider Aristotle's assertion that what determines the categories is whether the interests of the ruler or the interests of the governed are primary, thus determining whether the form of government is corrupted or not, as he writes:

> It is clear then that those constitutions that aim at the common advantage are in effect rightly framed in accordance with absolute justice, while those that aim at the rulers' own advantage only are faulty, and are all of them deviations from the right constitutions; for they have an element of despotism, whereas a city is a partnership of freemen.[19]

Aristotle's claims here could be interpreted, through a Jouvenelian lens, as criticism of any order which employs Jouvenelian means of centralisation. Such orders, in aligning with the periphery so as to disregard the intermediaries—the "community of freemen"—are recognised by Aristotle as acting in a coercive manner, utilising the periphery as a means to enforce their unilateral rule.

As for the other element of Aristotle's scheme, that of numbers, we are, again, left with a lack of clarity. Whilst the government of one is simple enough, Aristotle leaves us with no means of determining how many people constitute the government of

18 "In Greece, during the sixth century, they succeeded generally in procuring leaders; not wishing to call them kings, because this title implied the idea of religious functions, and could only be borne by the sacerdotal families, they called them tyrants.
Whatever might have been the original sense of this word, it certainly was not borrowed from the language of religion. Men could not apply it to the gods, as they applied the word king; they did not pronounce it in their prayers. It designated, in fact, something quite new among men—an authority that was not derived from the worship, a power that religion had not established. The appearance of this word in the Greek language marks a principle which the preceding generations had not known—the obedience of man to man." Coulanges, *The Ancient City*, 231.
19 Aristotle, *Politics*, 205.

the few, nor the government of the many. Both of these elements of the political categories—the concerns of the rulers and the numbers in government—pose serious problems, none of which are resolved in the modern period. The strongest attempt to do so is furnished in the shape of Robert Michels' work *Political Parties*, and what is striking about Michels' work is that despite having recourse to modern sociological resources and statistics, he still cannot provide a coherent definition of any category. For Michels, the issue of character is no longer a factor in defining the categories, which seems to be an attempt to remove any qualitative criteria, in line with modern sensibilities. Instead, Michels relies on statistical cut-off points as the means to differentiate government types.

In his preface, Michels defines monarchy: "[t]he most restricted form of oligarchy, absolute monarchy, is founded upon the will of a single individual."[20] But we are still left with confusion as to what oligarchy consists of, as Michels does not invoke character or wealth as a defining feature. This definition also makes no sense, since he is implying that rule by one person can be an oligarchy. Michels' confusing definitions continue in the following passage on oligarchies:

> The democratic external form which characterizes the life of political parties may veil from superficial observers the tendency towards aristocracy, or rather towards oligarchy, which is inherent in all party organisation."[21]

So, we see that Michels cannot clearly differentiate aristocracy from oligarchy, and slides between the two in the same sentence because from a quantitative angle, stripped of the extra categorisation of character, there is no difference. This also means that rule by one person can be monarchy, oligarchy, or aristocracy. On the question of aristocracy and democracy, the statistical nature of their difference is, again, demonstrated in the following passage where Michels quotes Rousseau's government classification in *Le Contrat Social*:

---

20 Robert Michels, *Political Parties: A Sociological Study of the Oligarchical Tendencies of Modern Democracy* (Batoche Books: Ontario, 2001), 7.
21 ibid., 13.

> We know today that in the life of the nations the two the-
> oretical principles of the ordering of the state are so elastic
> that they often come in reciprocal contact, "for democracy
> can either embrace all of the people or be restricted to half
> of them; aristocracy, on the other hand, can embrace half the
> people or an indeterminately smaller number." Thus the two
> forms of government do not exhibit an absolute antithesis,
> but meet at that point where the participants in power num-
> ber fifty per cent."[22]

What materially differentiates a government by 51% of the population from one by 50% of the population is not entirely clear.
Neither is the difference between an aristocracy of 50% of the
population and a democracy of 50% of the people clear, as the
question of character has been left out. What we are left with
is a situation in which 50% participation in government can be
democracy, aristocracy, or oligarchy, by Michels' own definitions.
Clearly, this is unsatisfactory.

More modern definitions of the political categories are even
less robust than Michels', and seem to possess no overall logical structure. The Wikipedia entry for democracy which, given
Wikipedia's centrality as a public information source, we can take
as the gold standard for our current definition, cites the political
scientist Larry Diamond in defining democracy as follows:

> [D]emocracy consists of four key elements: a political sys-
> tem for choosing and replacing the government through free
> and fair elections; the active participation of the people, as
> citizens, in politics and civic life; protection of the human
> rights of all citizens; a rule of law, in which the laws and
> procedures apply equally to all citizens.[23]

Here, we see that there is no longer an attempt to present democracy in some robust statistical way. Instead, at first glance, the various elements of this definition would seem somewhat arbitrary
and not directly connected; however, on closer examination they
do, indeed, prove to be connected, though not in a way which is
beneficial to Diamond's definition: the common thread in all four

22 Michels, *Political Parties*, 8.
23 *Wikipedia*, s.v. "Democracy," last modified March 6, 2019. https://en.wikipedia.
org/w/index.php?title=Democracy&oldid=886392760 (accessed March 9, 2019).

aspects of this modern definition of democracy is that they are historical cultural products of the Jouvenelian mechanism. Take, for example, the presence of elections, and the demand for all citizens to participate in politics and civil life. This is an essential part of centralising political systems, as these systems must shroud themselves in the equalisation and liberation of the individuals of society in order to reach the level of centralisation that they do. The primary Power, as we have seen extensively so far, must present its actions and its rule in a guise that hides the true nature of this relationship if it is to centralise effectively. As for the third criterion—the protection of human rights—this has no immediately comparable element in the classical categories at all. However, from the Jouvenelian angle, there is a connecting thread in that this is merely the latest in a long line of individualising thought systems that assist power expansion. In chapter 4, we saw that the development of human rights has a distinct link to the Jouvenelian mechanism of power expansion, and its inclusion in a political category according to which our social order defines itself should not surprise us at all. I have no doubt that Professor Diamond is in no way aware of this, but is, instead, merely describing the political landscape within which he resides. That these human rights arose as a development in furtherance of the centralisation of Power demonstrates, yet again, the way in which thought is shaped by power, and subsequently becomes relegated to the background and taken as objective reality.

Finally, the fourth criterion—the addition of rule of law—gives us a key insight into the nature of the connection between impersonal systems of governance and the success of this Jouvenelian centralising Power. Just as with the advent of coinage and money more broadly, the role of law in governance, particularly of written law, is to provide a means of enabling widespread control by a primary Power centre.

Diamond's definition of democracy would, therefore, seem to be a curious amalgamation of various measures and developments produced by the Jouvenelian expansion of Power. It seems to represent the accumulation of successful conceits that this expansion is not an expansion, but instead, an elevation of all to equality. This is not surprising, as what we see throughout the entirety of the modern development of democracy is a gradually, but perceptibly, increasing sophistication in presenting the primary Power's expansion as a spontaneous liberation and equalisation of the individual. This concept of democracy, a concept which has proven so useful to Power, is clearly a shroud for centralisation, and not a useful theoretical category.

From a Jouvenelian angle, it would seem that the political categories do not function as particularly useful tools for understanding political developments, and do more to bring about confusion and to hide the structures of power than they do to help us explain the nature of these structures. These categories systematically fail to take into account the Jouvenelian mechanism, and in so doing, they stand at odds with the observations and conclusions to be drawn from this mechanism, a mechanism which clearly provides a far fuller and more faithful account of the development of power structures.

VII

CORPORATIONS

As we have seen in previous chapters, across many disciplines there is a persistent and pervasive lack of awareness of the role played by structures of authority in cultural developments, and this has been exacerbated by the structural centralisation that underpins modernity. One key element of this process is the supposed distinction between the private and public spheres of existence, a concept which has become a core constituent of modern political reality. On one side of this distinction is the public realm of governance, and on the other is the private realm which is comprised of the individuals in society and other elements such as corporations.

Upon close inspection, this distinction between public and private is, yet again, revealed to be anything but timeless, maturing into its modern incarnation as late as the 19th century.[1] The ways in which these realms interact, and the border between them, differ between political ideologies, but that there is a public/private distinction is a constant. Operating within this tradition in a somewhat odd way are the various anarchisms that recognise this split and demand the total renunciation of the public realm. Note that these strains of anarchistic thought do not deny the validity

1   For a review of the history of this division, see Morton J. Horwitz, "The History of the Public/Private Distinction," *University of Pennsylvania Law Review*, Vol. 130 (1982): 1423–28, https://www.jstor.org/stable/3311976.

of these categorisations; they simply demand the abolishment of one of them.

This distinction creates a situation wherein it becomes evident, as it does in modernity, that the impact of authority on the very makeup (epistemological, linguistic, ethical, psychological, etc.) of the agents in this society goes unrecognised. The individuals in society, and society itself, have come to be understood as natural and spontaneous, but ultimately ordered (Locke) or disordered (Hobbes); but in any case, this private realm is not seen as intrinsically connected to authority—an authority which is, therefore, external to it, and must be created. As a result, we have governance, civil society, and, in more recent times, we also have the development of something which has been called an "economy." The definition of an economy, as with all of these concepts born and sustained by structural conflict, typically differs according to time and context; but overall, these various definitions tend to agree that the economy is, in some sense, an autonomous area of production, trade, and consumption, devoid of greater meaning. The concept of the economy is usually attributed to Adam Smith, but the French physiocrats predate him, and developed a number of concepts fundamental to his thought, especially the idea of an arena of natural liberty comprised of individuals that operate independent of authority.

From any angle but that of the Jouvenelian model, it would seem odd that the economic order would be a development of the physiocrats. It is a matter of record that the physiocrats wished to put the king of France into a position that could best be described as that of an oriental despot, and that they prized an agricultural society. So great was the influence of Confucius and the Chinese imperial system on François Quesnay that he has been labelled the "Confucius of Europe."[2] Quesnay even went so far as to propose the widespread adoption of Chinese institutions, and wrote a book on the topic entitled *Le Despotisme de la Chine*. The creation of such an order was supposed to allow the existence of a *laissez faire* economic realm, within which a quasi-natural order under the benevolent guidance of this despotic centralised monarchy could flourish unencumbered by the aristocracy and

2   Murray N. Rothbard, *Economic Thought Before Adam Smith: An Austrian Perspective on the History of Economic Thought, Volume I* (Aldershot: Elgar, 1995), 366.

the Church. In contrast with more modern accounts of *laissez faire* that practically do away with the role of government, the physiocrats were overt and enthusiastic supporters of this centralisation of power, on the premise that they believed that this order could not exist without this centralised governance. This reference to the need for a central political order is important to note, as this implies an order opposed to the distributed authority of the existing order of the period. Evidently, the physiocrats were producing ideas palpably in support of the monarch's court as the sole authority within the power structures of France. In recognising that the physiocrats were heavily connected to this centralisation, we can avoid the mistake of believing that mercantilism—the system opposed by the physiocrats—was the favoured system of the monarchy, and that the physiocrats were in some way anti-monarchical. Quesnay, the fountainhead of this school of thought, was a physician in the court of King Louis XV, and could hardly have produced his work if it was in any way unpalatable to the King's court.[3] Given this, we should be unsurprised to find the following line of argument from a notable physiocrat:

> Le Trosne argued, for example, that the absolute monarchy had tamed the nobility and presented royal justice to the people as "a guaranteed refuge and a shelter, which is always open, against violence and oppression." Moreover, achieving autonomy from the nobility, the absolute monarchy established "the most solid constitution, the one most appropriate to administering the laws of the [natural] order."[4]

The unmistakable conflict between the monarchy and the subsidiary structures of the nobility, here referred to as being for the

---

3 By comparison, Rothbard notes that Quesnay published under pseudonyms because "political economy was dangerous in that age of absolutism and censorship." Rothbard, *Economic Thought*, 366. The implication being that Quesnay's thought was, in some sense, subversive to the court. Rather, it seems likely that Quesnay's thought was warmly welcomed by the court; however, its directness and implications had the potential to create friction in the order of the time, particularly with regards to the aristocracy and clergy. That Quesnay became influential and even had one of his pupils, Anne Robert Jacques Turgot, installed as the *Controller-General of Finances* is instructive as to the value of his thought to the King's Court.

4 David McNally, *Political Economy and the Rise of Capitalism: A Reinterpretation* (Berkeley: University of California Press, 1988), 125.

benefit of the "people," is purely Jouvenelian.

The next step in the development of the concept of the modern economy was the introduction of this anarchistic ontology into English thought in the form of Adam Smith's *The Wealth of Nations*. Smith's work would come to the fore with the Anti-Corn Law movement of the 19th century, and, in light of this, it would be worthwhile to analyse briefly this movement to see if it doesn't also mirror the physiocrats' success on being supported by a centralising Power.

In 1839, the Anti-Corn Law League, espousing Adam Smith's economic thought, was created in Manchester, England, with the express purpose of pressuring the British government into repealing the Corn Laws which concerned restrictions on the importation of corn. The image passed down to us of the Anti-Corn Law League is that of a brave David, representing free trade, fighting against the Goliath of vested interests in the form of the landed aristocracy; yet, the funding figures for the movement and its opposition belie this. By 1845, the Anti-Corn Law League had managed to generate an annual fund of £250,000. In the same year, the League's most prominent group managed to raise a mere £2,000 to fund its activities.[5] This vast funding glut for the League was not supplied by the working poor in whose name it was supposedly speaking, but by a financial elite centred on the cotton textile manufacturing sector.[6] In the following year, 1846, funding ceased due to the successful repeal of the Corn Laws, which rendered the movement superfluous, and which put the agitators out of paid positions, as Anderson and Tollison note:

> The League dissolved basically because by 1846 its financial support had begun to dry up (McCord [1968], p.204). The League leaders and agitators did not suddenly lose interest in political issues, but many of them lost pay checks as employees in League offices.[7]

5 Cheryl Schonhardt-Bailey, *From the Corn Laws to Free Trade: Interests, Ideas, and Institutions in Historical Perspective* (Cambridge: MIT Press, 2006), 13.
6 Gary M. Anderson and Robert D. Tollison Bd. "Ideology, Interest Groups, and the Repeal of the Corn Laws," *Zeitschrift für die gesamte Staatswissenschaft / Journal of Institutional and Theoretical Economics*, 141, H.2. (June 1985): 201–02, https://www.jstor.org/stable/40750831.
7 Anderson and Tollison, "Repeal of the Corn Laws," 207–08.

It was this Anti-Corn Law movement that obtained the support of centralising Power in the form of parliament, and not the agricultural elite who were sliding into irrelevance. This thought system was clearly a weapon in a fight over political centralisation against an intransigent nobility.

Both the physiocrats and the Anti-Corn Law League are clear examples of idea systems being thrust into prominence by patrons, only to be abandoned when they are no longer needed, or when the patrons are no longer in power. In the case of the physiocrats, this patron was the French monarchy; in the case of the free trade advocates of the Anti-Corn Law League, this was the British Parliament—or, rather, a dominant industrial section of the British parliament headed by Prime Minister Robert Peel. Even though Peel was not directly connected to the League, he was perfectly happy to align with it when it suited him in his centralising efforts, and his advocacy of centralisation can be seen in the various policies he pursued, such as the Income Tax Act (1842), the first ever imposition of an income tax in peacetime. Peel, famously, was also behind the creation of the modern police force with his introduction of the Metropolitan Police Act (1829), hence "Bobby," the colloquial British term for policeman, in reference to Peel's given name. This all stands rather at odds with the individualism and liberty of free trade that is the hallmark of Adam Smith's economics—but from the Jouvenelian angle, it makes perfect sense. Expansive Power always promotes anarchistic appeals to the individual while it is expanding its own reach further into the order in question. The anarchistic claims are applicable to other power centres, but not to the centralising Power centre itself. The logic of an expansive government apparatus promoting anarchistic thought of this kind is also found when we move into the 20th century with the full development of the concept of an economy in the contemporary sense. Here, we find the progressive regimes of the British Empire and the United States on the scene, and in the process of another great wave of centralisation.

As part of the expansion of federal governance by Franklin Delano Roosevelt's government, the American progressive elite began to develop a number of claims regarding the scientific management of society which were mirrored in the British

Empire, something we shall see in more detail in chapter 8 with the development of political science. To this end, a Dr. Steven Kuznets was tasked by the Department of Commerce to develop a way to quantify the productivity of US industry in order to assist the federal government in understanding the causes of the Great Depression.[8] In response, Kuznets developed the concept of Gross National Product (GNP), which would be superseded by Gross Domestic Product (GDP) in 1944.[9] The concept of something called the "economy" that could be measured by GDP then became common usage. Another way to frame this narrative is to point out that this was a centralising Power centre expanding its reach and promoting a mode of thought which lent an air of scientific legitimacy to this expansion. The removal of subjective elements is a major necessity in this task, so this objective, apolitical, and measurable "economy" was carved out of the order as part of this process.

At this point, this development encountered a major problem in that the corporation—the cornerstone of modern commerce—does not cohere with the concept of an economy: the exemption of the corporation from the logic of free trade and individual autonomy became a pressing intellectual problem. The corporation had, therefore, to be explained in a manner that would warrant its existence within this anarchistic scheme, and this was provided by Ronald Coase's celebrated explanation for the existence of the firm. In *The Nature of The Firm*, Coase attempted to explain why organisations in the form of the corporation come to be, given that "it is usually argued that co-ordination will be done by the

8   U.S. Senate, *In Response to Senate Resolution No. 220 (72nd Cong.) A Report on National Income, 1929–32, (Calendar Day, January 4), 1934.* 73rd Congress, 2nd Session, 1934, S. Doc. 124. Washington: GPO, 1934. https://fraser.stlouisfed.org/scribd/?title_id=971&filepath=/files/docs/publications/natincome_1934/19340104_nationalinc.pdf.
9   Of interest is the biographical information supplied in Philipp Lepenies' book, *The Power of a Single Number: A Political History of GDP*. Kuznets, apparently, was tasked by the Bolsheviks with heading a department in the Bureau of Labor Statistics before his family immigrated to the US. This points towards similarities in governmental structures and techniques between these two supposedly opposite orders. Furthermore, Lepenies correctly identifies the key role played by philanthropic foundations in financing empirical attempts at creating a social science. Philipp Lepenies, *The Power of a Single Number: A Political History of GDP* (New York: Columbia University Press, 2016), 58–59.

price mechanism,"[10] or, in other words, to explain why we have a firm at all if the market can organise us in an individual-based, spontaneous, contractual manner by the use of the price mechanism. Coase's answer to the problem was to claim that in some instances organisation without the price mechanism is more cost effective. Coase is to be commended, because in his paper he makes his premises very clear: he takes the concept of the "specialized exchange economy" as a starting point, and establishes that he is considering man in light of Adam Smith's anthropological account. This, however, does not excuse Coase from failing to recognise that the concept of an economy is intrinsically linked with centralising Power, and is not a brute fact from which we can reason.

The contractual theory of the corporation, based as it is on the economic individual that underpins Coase's account, was taken even further in the 20th century by the Chicago School of Law and Economics, headed by Milton Friedman. The Chicago School began to popularise a theory asserting that the business corporation is merely a nexus of contracts between individuals, something also known as the "contractual" or "aggregate" theory of the corporation.[11] This is in stark opposition to the "artificial" theory which holds that the corporation is a creation of the state. There is a third version, the "real" theory, which holds that the corporation is an entity that is real, yet separate from the state and formed by individuals;[12] but this is, in essence, a weaker version of the aggregate theory, in that these two theories consider the corporation to be formed from a ground up process without reference to authority. This ontological claim precludes the corporation from being created by law, and places it firmly within the realm of spontaneous civil society, or the "economy." We can see

10   R.H. Coase, "The Nature of the Firm," *Economica, New Series*, Vol. 4, Issue 16 (November 1937): 388, https://doi.org/10.1111/j.1468-0335.1937.tb00002.x.
11   For an account of the actions of the Chicago School, see David Ciepley, "Beyond Public and Private: Toward a Political Theory of the Corporation," *American Political Science Review*, Vol. 107, No.1 (February 2013): 139–58.
12   For an overview of the various theories of the corporation, see Henry N. Butler, "The Contractual Theory of the Corporation," *George Mason University Law Review*, Vol. 11, No. 4, (Summer 1989): 99–123. Also, see Reuven S. Avi-Yonah, "The Cyclical Transformations of the Corporate Form: A Historical Perspective on Corporate Social Responsibility," *Delaware Journal of Corporate Law*, Vol. 30, No. 3 (2005): 767–818, https://dx.doi.org/10.2139/ssrn.672601.

this clearly in Friedman's *Capitalism and Freedom*,[13] where we find Friedman making the following claim:

> Fundamentally, there are only two ways of co-ordinating the economic activities of millions. One is central direction involving the use of coercion—the technique of the army and of the modern totalitarian state. The other is voluntary co-operation of individuals—the technique of the market place.[14]

The reader should note that Friedman has made a glaring omission in this passage, as he has simply put forward the market as the Western model. Of course, he does correct himself in later pages when he concedes that:

> The existence of a free market does not of course eliminate the need for government. On the contrary, government is essential both as a forum for determining the "rules of the game" and as an umpire to interpret and enforce the rules decided on.[15]

But this means his initial statement regarding the "two ways of co-ordinating the economic activities of millions" should be adjusted, and instead of positing the "market place" as the opposite of "central direction involving the use of coercion—the technique of the army and of the modern totalitarian state," it should be "the market place *under the control of the liberal state.*" This makes clear the usefulness of anarchistic thinkers such as Friedman to centralising Power. Government becomes a public "forum" and an "umpire" in service to this private free market, as opposed to being an actor forcing the concept of a "free market" into existence, just as a corporation is rationalised away as a matrix of individuals.[16] In framing the corporation as the result of this spontaneous

13 It is worth noting that Friedman makes a passing reference to the phenomenon of the Jouvenelian power conflict when he writes: "If the central government gains power, it is likely to be at the expense of local governments. There seems to be something like a fixed total of political power to be distributed." Milton Friedman and Rose D. Friedman, *Capitalism and Freedom* (Chicago: University of Chicago Press, 2002), 16.

14 ibid., 13.

15 ibid., 15.

16 The reader should also note the geopolitical influence in relation to the suc-

individualism, what the Chicago School was doing was making the role of authority in society opaque and unaccountable. In the contractual theory, the role of the corporation as an arm of governance becomes unchained from any sort of limits. The result, as David Ciepley notes, was that:

> The corporation became a pure creature of the market rather than a creature of government, exempting it from any duty to the public, or accountability to the public, or even publicity to the public, and rendering it eligible for a raft of constitutional rights, including electioneering rights.[17]

This neoliberal model of the modern business corporation is, however, wrong, and is wrong in strikingly obvious ways. The formation of a corporation results from the granting of recognition of personhood by a legal system. This institution—a legal entity recognised by authority—is then granted certain rights which include the ability to own property, the ability to enter into contracts and transactions, the limitation of liability of the human agents of the company to any losses incurred by the company, and the ability to issue shares. We can return again to Ciepley, who notes that:

> A charter formally ordains a corporation and, as part of this, expressly ordains and authorizes a board of directors, usually with members listed by name, to manage corporate assets, hire employees, define their duties, and generally conduct the corporation's affairs (Corporate Laws Committee 2005, §8.01, §3.02). It also expressly authorizes the board to issue stock up to a specified amount (Corporate Laws Committee 2005, §6.01). All this happens before there are any shares or shareholders. Given this sequence of events, it is clear that the government charter, and not the shareholder, creates and authorizes the board.[18]

The share that the shareholder owns is not a claim of ownership of the company; instead, it is a financial instrument which grants

cess of the Chicago School's thought, as it seems that a major reason for the patronage it enjoyed from the American government and foundations was its staunch anti-communist, liberal stance.

17 Ciepley, "Beyond Public and Private," 140.
18 ibid., 150.

certain rights, such as a potential dividends, voting rights, and some claim to the company's assets in the event of bankruptcy, though there are many classes of shares with varying rights.

It is quite obvious that the corporation is not a spontaneous creation of individual shareholders, and this is even more obvious in the case of non-profit corporations, such as tax-exempt foundations or universities which don't have shareholders. However, it must be noted that the example of the university provides us with an interesting situation in that the university can neither be explained by the artificial theory of the business corporation, nor can it be explained by the aggregate theory or the real theory. Whereas the business corporation and the charitable foundation can be traced to charters granted by legal systems, the university, in its origins, cannot; but this does not mean that it formed spontaneously in the sense implied by neoliberal theory. We can see this if we look at the history of the University of Bologna, widely recognised as the first university.

The University of Bologna presents us with a problem in that its founding seems to clearly predate any legal charter. The formal date of 1088 given for its creation, that used by the university itself, is unlikely to be correct, and, instead, appears to be a politically influenced date. A committee headed by Italian nationalist poet Giosuè Carducci seems to have chosen this inauguration date of 1088 on the basis of there being a legal school in existence at this time, run by an eminent teacher by the name of Irnerius. As a result, an 800-year jubilee was held in 1888 to celebrate this date and, importantly, to promote national unity. This event was influenced by the desire to help impart historical legitimacy to the newly formed Italian nation. In 1988, this claim was defended in a booklet produced for the 900th anniversary of Bologna University, on the basis that Irnerius' teaching was independent of Bologna's religious schools, which, therefore, distinguished it as a university.[19] This is a shockingly bad argument, and it is quite telling that this is the very best argument that could be advanced in support of this position.

More serious attempts to understand the development of the University of Bologna concentrate on the development of student

---

19   Hilde Ridder-Symoens and Walter Rüegg, ed., *A History of the University in Europe* (Cambridge: Cambridge University Press, 1992), 5.

guilds as the basis for the University. The reason for the students having formed into guilds appears to be related to their foreign origin. The students, not being citizens of Bologna, did not qualify for the same rights that Bologna's citizens enjoyed, which left them in a vulnerable position. For example, it appears that in instances where a foreigner owed money to a citizen of Bologna and left without paying, this debt could be extracted from another person of the same origin.[20] The difficult position the students found themselves in led them to form a guild, and to begin acting in a collective manner.[21] Initially, these guilds were formed along national lines, but later these nationality-based guilds formed into a unified, collective student guild which was called a *universitas*.[22]

This interpretation of the development of the university clearly places the charter, which was granted by Frederick Barbarossa, after the formation of the university. This sequence of events could be taken as confirmation of the contractual or real theory of the corporation, but this would be a mistake. The students may have organised together prior to the granting of corporate personhood by law, but they did so through a form of organisation which was expressly accepted as legitimate by the prevailing authorities in Bologna, even if it may not have been codified in law. The guild was a perfectly acceptable means of organising in a collective manner throughout medieval Europe. This is an important point to make since the claim of spontaneous organisation implicit in both the contractual and real theory of corporations gives the impression that organisation prior to legal recognition is completely without reference to the political order of society. Such an organisation is considered spontaneous, when, even in this case, it clearly was not.

20 This "excise of reprisal against foreign scholars" was rescinded by Frederick Barbarossa in 1155 with the *Authentica Habita*, the effect of which, as Paolo Nardi notes, was to "extend the benefit of clergy *(privilegium fori)* already enjoyed by clerics to lay students, and to confirm an old imperial rule (which since it came from Justinian's *Omnem* constitution was well known to the masters of Bologna) empowering the bishop and professors of Berito to judge students of that city." Paolo Nardi, "Relations with Authority," in *A History of the University in Europe* (Cambridge: Cambridge Univ. Press, 1992), 78.
21 See Harold J. Berman, "The Law School at Bologna," in *Law and Revolution: The Formation of the Western Legal Tradition* (Harvard University Press, Cambridge, 1983), 122–26.
22 ibid., 123.

Written law was developed as a means of codifying judgements by monarchs or other forms of authority so that these judgements could be transmitted beyond the personal, but this does not mean that non-codified or unwritten judgements were not binding, and are not still binding. The form of a guild is itself an example of this; the formation of guilds depended on oaths and personal agreements, and not on paper contracts or written legal recognition. So, we can see that it is perfectly possible that a corporation could be formed prior to legal recognition, and yet could still be a product of the express or implicit acceptance of the authorities of the order within which it resides. Perhaps it would be anachronistic to label it a corporation in the modern sense, but nonetheless it was recognised as an abstract entity with privileges and rights accepted by authorities. This is a position which all modern theories of the corporation discount by default, and it is central to modernity that authority cannot have an impact on society beyond the legal, as governance has become synonymous with rule through law. This distinction is a prescriptive one, and not a descriptive one.

The example of Bologna University now provides the basis for an alternative interpretation of the corporation, one in which the corporation is the product of the express or implicit recognition of authority, regardless of formal legal incorporation. If the students had formed into an organisation that the government of Bologna opposed, then it would have resulted in action against this state of affairs—but it did not. Authority recognised the corporate nature of this organisation, and as a result, so did other members of society.

So, we can see that with all organisations within the modern world, there is a distinct and noticeable tension between the demands of a politically determined anarchistic thought system and the immediate practical realities of these organisations. These organisations exist, and could only exist, as a result of the acknowledgement of their specific characteristics by authorities. The tax-exempt foundation, for example, is dependent on allowing a great deal of capital to be managed by agents and recognised as such by law, and, therefore, by authority. This authority is also what grants its tax-exempt status. It is inconceivable that this supposed "nexus of contracts" could grant itself tax exemption, yet this belief is implicitly demanded by the modern theory of corporations.

The reason why I raise the issue of tax-exempt foundations in connection with corporations and universities is that while in some instances the characterisation of organisations as belonging to a private realm is a means to disempower them in relation to the centralised government apparatus, at other times it serves as a means to empower them. In instances where the formal government apparatus becomes encumbered by blocks to action, the utilisation of "non-" governmental institutions raises the tantalising prospect of acting in a unilateral fashion under the exceptionally effective disguise of a spontaneous actor. The reader will appreciate the relevance of this as we begin to look at more modern Jouvenelian developments, where it becomes patently obvious that US-based, tax-exempt foundations have been vehicles whereby centralisation of power has been achieved on a vast scale. We have previously noted their role in relation to human rights, but as we progress we shall see that their influence has extended into large areas of life—yet, they have generally been exempt from scrutiny in standard political theory because they have been recognised as private actors. They have been considered part of the inscrutable anarchistic realm, which has enabled them to act with impunity with the acquiescence of actors within authority. This we shall see in more detail in the following chapter as we trace the development of modern political science.

VIII

THE DEVELOPMENT OF POLITICAL SCIENCE

GIVEN that political science is the obvious rival of the Jouvenelian approach to understanding human orders, a comparison of these competing approaches would be fruitful. One of the most powerful comparisons to be made is in applying both approaches to a problem recognised by both disciplines, and then drawing a conclusion as to which of the accounts provides a better explanation. An excellent example is found in presenting competing explanations for the origin of political science itself. What becomes immediately apparent from this exercise is that political science has no clear explanation for its own origin; in fact, it cannot even offer a clear definition of itself. This is not to say that there have not been attempts to provide a history of political science; there have been many, but almost all recount the history as if it is some kind of rational progress of ideas in which one strain of thought has succeeded another by dint of its persuasiveness. There are, however, a minority of histories of political science which recognise that, in many ways, the discipline has developed as it has for structural reasons, and these accounts prove of far greater value than the first kind.[1] These histories have often noted the defini-

1 For examples of the recognition of the role of foundations and other factors

tive role that foundations and structures of authority have played, but, despite noting these facts, they have lacked a suitable model by which to interpret them—thus, they have proven incapable of presenting their histories in a robust way. We shall see that it is all very well for critics like Bern Berelson to note that Ford Foundation funding made and shaped behaviouralism, or for Bernard Crick to complain that the science of politics, as dominated by American practitioners, is but a "caricature of American liberal democracy,"[2] but such observations, on their own, are consigned to insignificance or are simply ignored by political scientists in general, as they are anomalous observations which do not factor into political science. By comparison, these observations from the likes of Berelson and Crick do, indeed, find themselves at home within the Jouvenelian model, indicating that this model can account for far more observable facts than can any current variant of political science.

Fundamental to the Jouvenelian approach is the necessity of approaching political science as a product of the interplay between different power centres within a given power structure, according to the parameters that we have set out in previous chapters. In practical terms, what we must be able to identify is both a patron of political science as well as a motivation for this patron to act in a way which accords with the power structure conflict of an expansive Power centre. Just such an account can, indeed, be provided when we trace the history of political science in its modern guise.

In identifying the patrons of political science, the first step is to establish the funding sources which have brought political science to cultural significance. To this end, we may note that political science, in its modern form as centred around the American Political Science Association (APSA), developed from the actions

---

such as ideological beliefs determining the success of variants of political science and related disciplines, see Mark Bevir, Shannon C. Stimson and Robert Adcock, *Modern Political Science: Anglo-American Exchanges Since 1880* (Princeton: Princeton University Press, 2007). See also the introduction to Nicolas Guilhot, *The Invention of International Relations Theory: Realism, the Rockefeller Foundation, and the 1954 Conference on Theory* (New York: Columbia University Press, 2011), 1–32.

2   James Farr, "The History of Political Science," *American Journal of Political Science*, Vol. 32, No. 4 (November 1988): 1176, https://www.jstor.org/stable/i310473.

and funding of American progressives in the early 20th century, and expanded a great deal in the post-war period. The engine that drove this development was the funding that these progressive elites brought into play through their control of tax-exempt foundations, many of the same ones which would later be used in the human rights and civil rights funding that we have seen in chapter 4, and will see in chapter 9. For example, the Social Science Research Council (SSRC) was brought into existence by funding from a cross-network of foundations, as noted in the Rockefeller archives entry for the SSRC, which reveals that:

> To support its work, the SSRC turned not to the U.S. government, whose support seemed more appropriate for the natural sciences, but to private foundations. For the first fifty years, well over three-quarters of the SSRC's funding was provided by the Russell Sage Foundation, the Ford Foundation, the Carnegie Corporation, and two Rockefeller philanthropies, the Laura Spelman Rockefeller Memorial and the Rockefeller Foundation. By the 1970s, however, funds for some special projects were obtained from federal agencies.[3][4]

This same cross-network of funding sources was responsible for all the major political science institutes and trends that came into being throughout the Anglo-American world in the 20th century, with paradigmatic examples being the foundation of the Council on Foreign Relations (CFR) in the United States and the Royal Institute of International Affairs (RIIA, AKA Chatham House) in the United Kingdom.[5] Funding came from the Ford Founda-

3 "Other Organizations, Social Science Research Council Archives, 1924–1990," Rockefeller Archive Center, accessed March 12, 2017. http://rockarch.org/collections/nonrockorgs/ssrc.php.
4 See also Dorothy Ross' assessment of the importance of Rockefeller funding in not only the USA, but also Europe in "Changing Contours of the Social Science Disciplines," in *The Cambridge History of Science: The Modern Social Sciences*, ed. Theodore M. Porter and Dorothy Ross (Cambridge: Cambridge University Press, 2003), 205–37.
5 For details on the various funding sources for the RIIA and CFR, see Carroll Quigley, "The Royal Institute of International Affairs" in *The Anglo-American Establishment: From Rhodes to Clivedon* (New York: Books in Focus, 1981), 182–97. In addition, see Peter Grosse, *Continuing the Inquiry: The Council on Foreign Relations From 1921 to 1996* (New York: Council on Foreign Relations Press, 1996). For further information on the financing provided by foundations and members of international finance in order to create and maintain these two institutes, see

tion, the Carnegie Foundation, and the Rockefeller Foundation, to name but a few.[6] The Ford Foundation, in particular, would prove to be the main catalyst for the development of political science in the post-WWII era, as Joan Roelofs notes in *Foundations and Public Policy: The Mask of Pluralism*:

> Somit and Tanenhaus estimate that during the 1950s and 1960s:
>
>> [T]he Ford complex provided 90 percent of the money channeled to political science by American philanthropic institutions.[7]

This initial funding from the likes of the Ford Foundation resulted in a positivistic political science being placed firmly in the driver's seat in Anglo-American academia.

Having now established the identity of the patrons of this political science, our next task is to explain the motivations and reasons behind the patrons' funding decisions. In addressing this problem, a document which details the motivations and beliefs that led to this elite's patronage would prove exceptionally useful. Fortunately, we have just such a document in the shape of the *Report of the Study for the Ford Foundation on Policy and Program*,[8] penned by Rowan Gaither at the behest of Henry Ford II in 1947. This document provides a summary of the cream of American elite thought at this point in time. As explained by the Rockefeller Archive Center, the commission for the report sought:

> "the best thought available" in government, business, education, health, natural sciences, and other fields to identify national and world problems to which the Foundation could respond with a large and well-defined program. Rather than

also Inderjeet Parmar, *Think Tanks and Power in Foreign Policy: A Comparative Study of the Role and Influence of the Council on Foreign Relations and the Royal Institute of International Affairs, 1939–1945* (Basingstoke: Palgrave Macmillan, 2004).
6 "Social Science Research Council Archives, 1924–1990," Rockefeller Archive Center, accessed March 12, 2017. http://rockarch.org/collections/nonrockorgs/ssrc.php.
7 Joan Roelofs, *Foundations and Public Policy: The Mask of Pluralism* (Albany: State University of New York Press, 2003), 42.
8 H.R. Gaither Jr., *Report of the Study for the Ford Foundation Policy and Program* (Detroit: Ford Foundation, 1949).

embarking on an academic exercise studying stacks of written data, the committee drew its conclusions from over one thousand interviews with notable figures as diverse as Walt Disney, Dwight D. Eisenhower, and Eleanor Roosevelt.[9]

This report resulted in the setting of a specific series of goals to which the Ford Foundation would devote its vast wealth, and the conclusion to which the commission came was that the foundation's activities should concentrate on the following five programs:

> Program Area One deals with the conditions of peace essential to democratic progress. Program Area Three is concerned with the economic bases of democracy, Program Area Four with its educational foundations, and Program Area Five with the conditions of personal life requisite for democratic self-realization.[10]

Program Area Two, meanwhile, was simply "[t]he strengthening of democracy."[11] From the above quote, the fifth category is not clear, however its chapter title of "Individual Behavior and Human Relations"[12] should make clear that it refers to social and political science.

One of the first things that needs to be brought to the reader's attention is that all five programs, including the "Individual Behavior and Human Relations" program, are framed specifically in relation to democracy. As we have seen in previous chapters, when we see the citation of democracy, what we are really seeing is the Jouvenelian expansion of primary Power. To confirm this requires us to examine the nature of democracy, as conceived by the American elite in this report, in order to confirm if it accords with the patterns of democracy that we have seen since its inception as a category in the Greek states. In this respect, the formulation of democracy in the report does not disappoint once we pierce through the convoluted language that Gaither uses to describe

9   Patricia Rosenfield and Rachel Wimpee, *The Ford Foundation: Constant Themes, Historical Variations*, Rockefeller Archive Center, 4–5, accessed March 9, 2019. https://rockarch.org/publications/ford/overview/FordFoundationHistory1936-2001.pdf.

10   Gaither Jr. *Report of the Study for the Ford Foundation*, 63.

11   ibid., 62.

12   ibid., 90.

it. The type of order that Gaither describes is clearly a centralised political structure in a direct relationship with individuals, as can be seen when Gaither writes the following of democracy:

> [O]ur political institutions do not themselves constitute democracy. They can only establish a climate in which democracy may flourish...
> [...]
> Clearly, therefore, in speaking of democracy, the Committee is not thinking merely of the form of our institutions and organisations, which are but means or instruments for men's requirements.[13]

This definition diverts attention away from the institutions which are creating this order, and paints them as being at the service of the individual; but this is merely a matter of emphasis. It is a conceit that there is a spontaneous and anarchistic society which is merely being served by these institutions rather than being created and held in equilibrium by them.

The discussion of the meaning of the term "democracy" is taken up in more detail in a later section entitled the "Need to Clarify the Meaning of Democracy,"[14] wherein it is candidly acknowledged that democracy as a term has no objective, set definition. This lack of definition does not stop Gaither from immediately entering into discussion of advancing democracy's frontiers, the meaning of which is specified as the advancement of the individual in whatever guise can be found. Gaither clearly has an acute understanding of the role that democracy plays in the promotion of the individual, and that settling on a definition of democracy linked to institutions is pointless indeed—an understanding which accords precisely with the Jouvenelian interpretation of the development of the term "democracy." Gaither refers to this constant emancipation of the individual as "democracy's ideological frontier,"[15] which is clearly synonymous with "progress":

> This frontier has been continuously moving since the founding of our country. All basic democratic concepts must expand by interpretation to embrace new situations and to

13 Gaither Jr. *Report of the Study for the Ford Foundation*, 20–21.
14 ibid., 64–67.
15 ibid., 65.

resolve the social issues which arise out of changing condi-
tions. For example, the principles of individual freedom and
self-government have moved past the issues of slavery and
universal suffrage to such current frontiers as the political
participation of racial minorities.[16]

Gaither is obviously unable to account for this trend on his own
terms, just as modern thinkers, as a whole, have been unable to
do. The result has been that modernity, and the advancement of
modern culture, is often explained with reference to metaphysical
crutches such as "progress" or "the arc of history," or, in Gaither's
case, the rather mysterious "democratic frontier." We have no reason to accept this unclear modelling, and instead, we can simply
place the emphasis back on the institutions rather than on the
individual. In doing so, we can see that Gaither is narrating the
centralisation of the United States and the resultant claims which
have been advanced to justify this centralisation—even if he does
not envision it in these terms.

This centralisation in the period in which Gaither is writing,
and of which he is the agent, is clearly not being conducted solely
through formal political institutions. The elites' move to utilise
such institutions as the Ford Foundation indicates issues with the
political system of the time that were stifling the elites presiding
over this system in their political aims. Recall that it is central
to the Jouvenelian system that the centralising elite of a given
society must revert to anarchistic claims, and to the elevation of
the individual specifically, in instances of political conflict or in
the presence of barriers to the liberty of the centralising Power. In Medieval Europe, the conflict between Church, monarchy,
and nobility provided the engine for such developments, and we
would need to locate a similar set of problems in the society within which Gaither resides. We can gain insight into these problems
when we note that in the report Gaither specifically dismisses
extant American institutions as being the embodiment of democracy, and even goes so far as to write that:

> To identify present forms too closely with democratic ideals
> is to make idols of the forms, thereby hindering their im-
> provement for the service of mankind.

16   Gaither Jr. *Report of the Study for the Ford Foundation*, 65–66.

> In times of uncertainty many people tend to resist change, in the illusion that democracy and its institutions are made more secure by an unchanging order. This, we believe, strikes at the very heart of democracy by denying to it the right to grow. For democracy's greatest strength lies in its ability to move constantly forward in action toward the increasing fulfilment of people's needs and the greater achievement of its goals.[17]

What Gaither is really saying here is that political centralisation, and the advancement of the individual by this political centralisation, need not continue through the formal institutions which currently exist, and that, as a result, the development of new institutions which are able to operate more freely is necessary. This is the role of the Ford Foundation. In later sections this is explained in more direct ways, shorn of the language of democracy. In the section labelled "Direct Aids to Policy Makers,"[18] we begin to see the reasons why Gaither and the American elite have become so enamoured with the so-called "private" foundations, as it is made clear that the formal structures of the United States and the United Nations are seen as active hindrances to the actions of this elite. The recurring complaint in this section is that the political system, with its checks and balances, and with its various branches, acts as an impediment to goals which this elite wishes to accomplish. Writing of the difficulty of information exchange, Gaither states:

> The Congress and many of its major committees, the President and his Executive Office, all executive departments, and most of the independent agencies and regulatory commissions play various roles in international political and economic affairs. Many obstacles block the exchange of information among these bodies on any given issue; even to assemble pertinent information about the procedural and organizational problems involved is difficult, since each agency is sensitive about its jurisdictional privileges.[19]

This reference to the constitutionally dictated structure of the US

17   Gaither Jr. *Report of the Study for the Ford Foundation*, 21.
18   ibid., 55–61.
19   ibid., 55–6.

government in less than glowing terms is repeated at a number of points, and is often cited as a primary impetus for the development of the Foundation. Writing on pg. 58, Gaither states:

> A foundation can support studies and analyses by special committees, individuals, or research institutes where official agencies are hampered by foreign or domestic political considerations or by the appearance of self-interest. It can assist in the analysis of fundamental issues or policies where our Government or the United Nations may lack objectivity, talents, or time. It can, in appropriate situations, make available to the State Department or to the United Nations expert knowledge and judgement on important subjects.[20]

The entire justification for the republican system is that the presence of other branches of government are designed to act as a check, thereby supposedly ensuring good governance, and constraining any one branch from becoming overly powerful. What Gaither is complaining of here is precisely what this political system was designed to do. This disdain for political barriers is stated plainly when Gaither writes:

> At every level of government—federal, state, and local—we entrust control of policy to executive officials and to legislators. Successful self-government requires that the decisions of these persons express the will of the people on economic, social, and political needs. In practice, legislative enactments and administrative decisions often reflect the special interests of particular groups rather than the welfare of the public. Too many decisions, moreover, fail to be effective because the machinery of government is inadequate or inefficient.[21]

This disdain is not simply limited to the republican structure, but is also directed at the electoral system—this is made clear when Gaither writes of the need for the presence of the foundation in the process of advancing social change by, again, pushing the "democratic frontier." Gaither makes the claim that:

> A foundation may enter controversial areas boldly and with

20 Gaither Jr. *Report of the Study for the Ford Foundation*, 58.
21 ibid., 31.

> courage as long as it maintains a nonpartisan and nonpolit-
> ical attitude and aids only those persons and agencies moti-
> vated by unselfish concern for the public good.[22]

Not only, then, are the elite on behalf of whom Gaither writes disdainful of the political barriers of formal governance, but also of the political conflicts required by the electoral system. In response, it can be seen in this document that they have settled upon the presentation of their actions as being apolitical, neutral, and utterly centred on the public good, which has allowed them to advance within the accepted norms of the order within which they operate. This behaviour is precisely in line with the Jouvenelian mechanism. The political structure, and the constraints which it has placed on the governing centre, have determined the shape of the concepts that have been brought forward in the service of its expansion.

If we accept this interpretation, then it is clear that the foundations have become a means of political centralisation supplied with an even greater level of camouflage than that provided to recognised republican governance structures. The foundation—in not even being accepted as part of governance, despite actively being involved in governance—has become an institution exceptionally well-adapted for the expansion of Power. Key to this is the foundation's ability to present itself as a private and impartial entity, and Gaither says as much when he writes:

> A great foundation possesses an extraordinary stature in the
> public mind. By law, as well as by its charter, it is dedicated to
> human welfare. Its responsibility is to the public as a whole.
> In political and social issues it cannot be partisan. This very
> nonpartisanship and objectivity gives to the foundation a
> great positive force, and enables it to play a unique role in
> the difficult and sometimes controversial task of helping to
> realize democracy's goals.[23]

Of course, if we change the reference to "democracy's goals" to "the American centralising elite's goals," then this passage becomes much clearer.

---

22 Gaither Jr. *Report of the Study for the Ford Foundation*, 67.
23 ibid., 23.

Having established the identity of the patrons of political science, and having followed the reasoning that these patrons have given for the actions they would take, it is clearly important for us to examine more closely the nature of this individual being promoted in Gaither's report. It is, indeed, the case that the individual is being promoted, as the section of the report that deals with political science specifically references the individual in its title, thereby making this individual the constituent unit, or atom, of this science. Unfortunately, Gaither does not offer an explicit definition of the individual, and one can only be gleaned from numerous sections of what is, at base, a theoretically confused report; and this theoretical confusion arises from the tension between the report's aim of outlining a vision of democratic governance, and the underlying assumption of the modern individual who does not necessarily need government. This tension can be noted when Gaither writes:

> While our ultimate concern is with the individual, it is clear that only in society can his full development take place. Modern man cannot forsake society in search of freedom; freedom, for him, exists only within and by means of the social order. Men are no freer than the arrangements and condition of society enable them to be [...] No longer can individuals, or nations, retreat into self-sufficiency. Men live together whether they want to or not; all are thrust, from birth, into an immense network of political, economic, and social relationships.[24]

The confusion in this passage is palpable. It seems that Gaither has in mind the modern individual that we have seen in earlier chapters, but he is trying to claim that the complexities of modern existence make this individual dependent on governance. This is, at base, a repetition of the overall structure of the social contract theory: there are individuals; these individuals cannot live as individuals for some reason or other; and because of this, they are now inescapably stuck with the necessity of governance. This individual of Gaither's is precisely the individual of political and social science which Charles Taylor recognises as having been derived from "social contract theories that emerged in the seventeenth

---

24 Gaither Jr. *Report of the Study for the Ford Foundation*, 19.

century with Grotius, Pufendorf, Locke and others,"[25] and which have become:

> ...moral sources for the view that human beings "start off as political atoms" capable of "disengagement" from the world around them which no longer has any "larger, meaningful order." Instead the individual is seen as the sovereign source of meanings and values. This in turn "yields a picture of the sovereign individual, who is 'by nature' not bound to any authority."[26]

This individual is the individual assumed as a given empirical fact by Gaither, just as it was assumed by all before him in the liberal tradition, and it is this empirical "fact" who is then burdened with numerous ethical constraints before this individual is even placed before the political science that is to study him.

In chapter 5, we noted that Alasdair MacIntyre's criticisms of the ethical projects of modernity largely correspond with the changes in institutions that have occurred within the Western world, and in this document we find that this inherited ethical confusion is present in precisely the ways that we would expect. Gaither and his brand of mid-20th century American progressivism is first justified on a consequentialist basis with appeals to naturalistic teleology in the form of claiming survival, improvement in living standards, and good health as rationales for its interpretation of human welfare.[27] Not content with simply appealing to naturalistic teleology, Gaither then goes on to appeal to a categorical imperative of sorts with the claim that:

> Basic to human welfare is the idea of the dignity of man— the conviction that man must be regarded as an end in himself, not as a mere cog in the mechanisms of society.[28]

This is then followed by a series of claims as to the nature of per-

---

25 Jason William Blakely, "Three Political Philosophers Debate Social Science: Leo Strauss, Alasdair MacIntyre, and Charles Taylor," PhD diss., (University of California, Berkeley, 2013), 93.

26 Blakely, "Three Political Philosophers," 93.

27 See Gaither Jr., "Chapter I, Human Welfare," in *Report of the Study for the Ford Foundation*, 17–24.

28 Gaither Jr. *Report of the Study for the Ford Foundation*, 17.

sonal freedom and rights, political freedom and rights, and social responsibility and the duty of service, which are, again, framed along the lines of a categorical imperative. Remarkably, what Gaither has done in this report is to establish human welfare, and, therefore, the ethical grounds of democracy, on not one basis, but on two bases which are mutually exclusive. A deontological system of ethics cannot be blended with a consequentialist system in the way that Gaither proposes—a consequentialist system is one wherein the results of an action determine its ethical status, whereas a deontological system is one which places importance on the act itself regardless of the result of the action. Regardless of this incoherence, at the heart of these ethical claims is the attempt to provide a framework for how individuals within a society of a specifically liberal character are to interact and live together. It is in the service of this ethical position that political science is supposed to provide insights in order to assist this democratic project. This is plainly an ideologically informed discipline with a political purpose, but it is being presented as a value-neutral science, and it is still conceived of as such today.

This democratic individualistic set of assumptions was subsequently unleashed on the world and formed the basis of modern empirical political science, initially under the name of behaviouralism. Erkki Berndtson, in a wide-ranging essay on the subject, notes that:

> Many have even argued that the whole concept of behavioralism came into use only because of the policy of foundations (Geiger 1988: 329). And Bernard Berelson seems to agree:
>
>> "What happened to give rise to the term? The key event was the development of a Ford Foundation program in this field. The program was initially designated 'individual behavior and human relations' but it soon became known as the behavioral sciences program and, indeed, was officially called that within the foundation. It was the foundation's administrative action, then, that led directly to the term and to the concept of this particular field of study." (Berelson 1968: 42)
>
> The foundation money created also a self-generat-

ing process which led to the recruitment of behavioralists. Because behavioralist projects were funded better than traditional ones, there were a larger supply of
behavioralists up for recruitment than others (Hacker
1959: 39-40). It is no wonder that some of the key
practitioners of behavioralism have been willing to
admit that "it was almost single-handedly the Ford
Foundation that did so much to legitimate empirical
social science" (Warren E. Miller in Baer, et al., eds.
1991: 242).[29]

Berelson, for the record, was the director of the Ford Foundation's
Behavioral Sciences Program between 1951 and 1957. We can
see, then, that the actions of the Ford Foundation, and of the
American elites in control of this foundation, proved decisive in
determining the shape and direction that political science took,
by virtue of controlling the funding that it received. This funding
acted as a selection mechanism for what were deemed to be acceptable assumptions for what constitutes a political science, and
what was deemed acceptable was an individualistic interpretation
of human orders in line with established liberal ideological assumptions.

Another means by which these foundations have had their role
hidden is the simple mechanism whereby any theorist developing
political thought critical of the role of foundations will clearly not
seek funding from the foundations, and would be unlikely to be
granted funding even if they did. As all traditions of thought are
implied to be acting on a field of total equality, with the implication that the success of any given one is due to intellectual superiority, the effectiveness of this process in hiding the foundations'
role is significant.

So, as we can see, the tools available to political scientists cannot offer a feasible explanation for the development of political
science; however, by utilising the Jouvenelian theoretical model,
we are able to offer just such an account, and one which takes into
account a great deal of information which political scientists are
unable even to recognise as relevant.

---

29   Erkki Berndtson, "Behavioralism: Origins of the Concept" (presentation, 17th
International Political Science Association World Congress, Seoul, Korea, August
17–21, 1997).

IX

THE LEFT AND RIGHT OF POLITICS

No account of modern political structures would be complete without an account of that persistent and chronic pathology of modern government that manifests itself as the left/right political distinction. The origins of this conception, rather pertinently for our model, date to the seating arrangements of the French National Assembly following the French Revolution. The various factions within the assembly self-sorted, so that on left side of the assembly sat the republicans, the forces of centralisation (consciously or not) who advocated widespread change and social levelling, and on the right sat the monarchists, the forces of decentralisation who sought to maintain the patterns of existence that obtained before the Revolution. From the Jouvenelian angle, this split was simply a recognition of the relation between the forces of centralisation and the equality and individualism which they espoused—an equality and individualism which, it must be remembered, was directed at the intermediary centres of the power structure. That they were centralising has, in modernity, been completely obscured. It is this central confusion which has rendered attempts to explain phenomena so problematic, and we can see this in detail when we attend to the structures of the relative political wings.

The left section of the political division is recognisable within our model as an expression of two parts of the Jouvenelian dynamic. The first element is the self-effacing centralising primary Power; the second element is the periphery whose claims to equality and individualism are being promoted. This marginalised periphery has ranged from simply the poor (who can be defined at will) to the proletariat, racial minorities, individuals outside of aristocratic society, LGBT persons, immigrants, women—the list is as varied as the makeup of the various structures. The key to this dynamic is that this marginalised peripheral element is promoted, and this promotion is a means whereby the centralising Power can undermine subsidiary centres of power and can expand its own power. As a result of the nature of this mechanism, the centralising elite are incentivised to hide their role, and often even convince themselves that they are merely the facilitators of the periphery's demands. Moreover, even in instances where the elites in question appear to wholeheartedly believe that they are not centralising or supporting centralised structures—such as, for example, with anarchists—it matters not, because this equality and individualism cannot exist without a centre, and so they assist this centre unwittingly. The two elements are intertwined and inseparable, but one can see the incredible power that can be attained by hiding, or by failing to understand, that this is so.

This underlying connection between the elite and the periphery explains why one can find otherwise incongruent stances on the left side of the spectrum: socialisms, anarchisms, communisms, liberalisms, etc. These various positions permit a sort of modularity in the Jouvenelian dynamic, in that, depending on the circumstances, the elites within society can, and will, ally with different peripheral groups at different times; the manner in which the broad left wing has developed over history is a testament to this. The purpose of centralising elites aligning with peripheral groups is that the positions taken by these groups represent various attacks on the extant intermediary power structures, and as such, represent valuable resources in the process of centralisation. Granted, some of these groups may direct these attacks against the centralising primary Power, but in this instance, the simple act of withdrawing support suffices to curtail these groups—political significance is a result of institutional existence, and it is the centralising Power that holds the reins of finance, organisational capability, and authority. This act of removing support is a direct demonstration of the selection effects of Power on culture. We find a clear and pertinent example of this dynamic in the American civil rights era when the elites of American structures of authority sponsored various black empowerment movements into prominence, movements which are generally accepted as left wing.

This civil rights era exists in modern consciousness as some kind of miraculous and spontaneous development. The various protests and the rise to prominence of such figures as Martin Luther King Jr. and Rosa Parks are often presented as having just happened according to some historical spirit. The reality is far more unsettling. We can get an immediate grasp of the situation when we consider the following speech delivered by Malcolm X, entitled *Message to the Grass Roots*. In this speech, Malcolm makes the accusation that the civil rights marches, as well as the major black actors in the movement, were funded by white elites. His speech claims that:

> A philanthropic society headed by a white man named Stephen Currier called all the top civil-rights leaders together at the Carlyle Hotel. And he told them that, "By you all fighting each other, you are destroying the civil-rights movement. And since you're fighting over money from white liberals, let us set up what is known as the Council for United Civil Rights Leadership. Let's form this council, and all the civil-rights organisations will belong to it, and we'll use it for fund-raising purposes."[1]

The money in question amounted to at least "[a] million and a half dollars,"[2] which, adjusted for inflation, would equal $12.46 million in 2019 dollars. In addition to this money, public relations support was supplied:

> [As] soon as they got the setup organized, the white man made available to them top public relations experts; opened the news media across the country at their disposal; and then

1 Malcolm X, "Message to the Grass Roots" (speech, King Solomon Baptist Church, Detroit, MI, November 10, 1963), TeachingAmericanHistory.org, accessed June 6, 2019, http://teachingamericanhistory.org/library/document/message-to-grassroots/.
2 ibid.

they begin [sic] to project these Big Six as the leaders of the march.[3]

This philanthropic institution referred to by Malcolm X was set up by Stephen Currier and his wife Audrey Bruce Currier (née Mellon) of the Mellon fortune. Civil rights leaders also received significant funding from the Ford Foundation and the Rockefeller Foundation, amongst other funding sources of the same kind. The level of elite support for this movement was substantial and definitive.

At this point, the reader should note that whilst Malcolm X is often feted as part of the civil rights movement, he was, nonetheless, cut off from this funding, since he advocated for far more militant action than the elite were willing to accept, and was far more doctrinaire in advocating the autonomous advancement of blacks than was Martin Luther King Jr. As such, Malcolm X was tolerated, but his views never rose to institutional significance because the financiers and suppliers of logistics did not back them. Instead, as the above speech makes clear, they funded other actors in this drama. The alliance between Nelson Rockefeller and Martin Luther King Jr., in particular, is an instructive demonstration of the mechanism. King received significant and repeated funding from Rockefeller throughout his career, from the provision of $25,000 to King's Gandhi Society for Human Rights ($201,000 in adjusted 2019 dollars),[4] to even receiving bail money.[5] In an interview with Vanity Fair in 2006, King's lawyer at the time, Clarence Jones, revealed that at one point Rockefeller provided bail funds for King's arrested followers in the amount of $100,000 ($830,000 in adjusted 2019 dollars). Jones is also quoted as agreeing with Malcolm X's assessment that the role of funding was central to the civil rights movement, stating that "Jewish Americans, along with a few guys like Rockefeller, financed the

3   Malcolm X, "Message to the Grass Roots".
4   Martin Luther King Jr. to Nelson A. Rockefeller, Monday, November 1, 1965, The King Center Archive, accessed March 28, 2017. http://thekingcenter.org/archive/document/letter-mlk-nelson-rockefeller.
5   *Stanford University King Encyclopedia*, s.v. "Rockefeller, Nelson Aldrich," accessed March 28, 2017. https://kinginstitute.stanford.edu/encyclopedia/rockefeller-nelson-aldrich.

civil-rights movement."[6]

Here, then, we see the dynamics of the left wing in play. We have an elite driving change in a self-effacing way under the cover of a call to equality or individualism. In this iteration, the elite operated from foundations and civil society groups as well as from government (specifically, federal government), and did so in a centralising way. This centralising can be seen insofar as the goal of the civil rights era was to promote the individual rights and equality of the black population against the laws and control at the state level which facilitated the centralising of governance at the federal level. An excellent example demonstrating this pattern is the famous Brown v. Board of Education of Topeka 1954 case. The National Association for the Advancement of Colored People (NAACP) actively brought this case into being, with the chief litigator becoming an Associate Justice of the Supreme Court himself in 1967.[7] The funding for the case was provided by liberal philanthropic foundations.[8] What is even more remarkable about this case is the unprecedented reliance by the court on social science testimony in making their decision. This testimony was cited as proving that there were scientific bases for the claim that segregation had a negative effect on the educational achievements of black students. While it is not our place to examine the scientific validity of the studies used, it is pertinent to point out that in chapter 8 we saw the provenance of this form of social science in the funding actions of the foundations, and here we find it being used by the very same actors in order to centralise power. We can even find in the *Report of the Study for the Ford Foundation* an express desire to turn this kind of "science" towards questions of minority tensions and race relations, just as it is being used here. It is, obviously, quite fortunate that the findings confirmed the assumptions of these elites.[9]

---

6   Douglas Brinkley, "The Man Who Kept King's Secrets," *Vanityfair.com*, April, 2006.   http://www.vanityfair.com/news/politics/2014/01/clarence-jones-martin-luther-king-jr-secrets.

7   Thurgood Marshall, the NAACP's chief counsel, went from working for a foundation and elite-supported institution to becoming a fixture of formal governance.

8   Walter Stephan and Joe R. Feagin, *School Desegregation: Past, Present, and Future* (New York: Plenum Press, 1980), 33–35.

9   Gaither Jr., *Report of the Study for the Ford Foundation*, 97.

To recap, the Brown v. Board 1954 case was brought to court with elite funding of legal costs, elite organisation to find plaintiffs, as well as "science" produced by the elite with elite funding, and it was then determined by the court that the opinions of the elite (of which the court were members) were in fact "scientifically" grounded and correct. The remarkably un-spontaneous nature of this case is palpable. The question is, then, why was this pantomime acted out in this manner? The answer, from a Jouvenelian angle, lies in the structure of the US government. President Truman had removed racial segregation in the armed forces in 1948,[10] but his ability to do so in the school system was limited by the fact that schools were under state control. The official route for altering this state of affairs was to get Congress to act under the 14th Amendment of the Constitution which senators would not have supported since segregation had broad electoral support. The route taken was a legal one in which we find a scheme of byzantine complexity involving various "private" actors such as foundations and the National Association for the Advancement of Colored People (NAACP). The link between the Truman presidency and the NAACP in this dynamic can be seen in the continual support that his presidency provided for its legal endeavours, and the support that he voiced for it.[11] The Brown v. Board case is also noteworthy for demonstrating the influence of geopolitical considerations on the centralising efforts of centres of power, something we shall return to in chapters 10 and 11. The Department of Justice issued a friend of the court brief in which it complained that "[r]acial discrimination furnishes grist for the Communist propaganda mills,"[12] which points towards there be-

---

10   Exec. Order. No. 9981 13 Fed. Reg. 4313 (July 28, 1948), https://www.archives.gov/federal-register/executive-orders/1948.html#9981.

11   Truman encouraged the Department of Justice to issue friends of the court briefs in a number of civil rights cases, and even addressed the NAACP's annual convention in June 1947, declaring that "[t]he extension of civil rights today means not protection of the people *against* the government, but protection of the people *by* the government [...] We must make the federal government a friendly, vigilant defender of the rights and equalities of all Americans. And again I mean all Americans." James T. Patterson, *Brown V. Board of Education: A Civil Rights Milestone and Its Troubled Legacy* (New York: Oxford University Press, 2001), 1.

12   To see this, we can turn to a *Reuters* article by Aryeh Neier which makes the following observations on the case in general, and in particular, on a friend of the court brief issued by Attorney General James P. McGranery of the Department of

ing a distinctly imperial flavour to American promotion of racial equality.

A similarly instructive example of the nature of the left is provided by more recent developments, this time in the form of the Black Lives Matter movement which came to prominence in 2014. The dynamic of this movement, a movement clearly left wing, maps precisely to the Jouvenelian model.

In the case of the Black Lives Matter movement, the federal government, again along with foundations, utilised the movement for reasons of power centre conflict and centralising. Their motivations and goals were varied, but all followed the same logic imposed by their relative positions within the Jouvenelian model. We can provide a first-hand account of the thinking of the actors involved in this development thanks to the leaking of a number of documents from the Open Society's May 2015 meetings. These documents contain passages detailing the motivations for various actors to capitalise on the Black Lives Matter protests occurring around this time, protests against the claimed targeting of black individuals as a result of supposedly systemic racism by American police forces. The federal government is cited as specifically seeking foundation support in their aim to reform the structure of the American police force. To this end, the foundations developed pressure groups and supplied the resources for organised protests to illuminate the supposedly poor treatment of the black population, which then lent support to justifying these police reforms.[13]

Justice: "The United States is trying to prove to the people of the world of every nationality, race and color, that a free democracy is the most civilized and most secure form of government yet devised by man.... The existence of discrimination against minority groups in the United States has an adverse effect upon our relations with other countries. Racial discrimination furnishes grist for the Communist propaganda mills." It also featured an excerpt from a letter by Secretary of State Dean Acheson, described as "an authoritative statement of the effects of racial discrimination in the United States upon the conduct of foreign relations." Aryeh Neier, "Brown v. Board of Ed: Key Cold War Weapon," *Reuters*, May 14, 2014. http://blogs.reuters.com/great-debate/2014/05/14/brown-v-board-of-ed-key-cold-war-weapon/.

13   See the May 7–8, 2015 Open Society U.S. Programs Board Meeting, where it is stated plainly that "[t]he federal government is seeking philanthropic support for a number of its initiatives. In addition to seeking support to advance the implementation of the recommendations of the Presidential Taskforce, the White House recently launched the Policing Data Initiative to explore how best to use data and technology to build trust, voice, and solutions to improve community po-

A further leaked document detailing meetings in October 2015 is even more pointed in its revelations than the earlier one. In this memo, we find the following rather remarkable passage:

> Recognizing the need for strategic assistance, the U.S. Programs Board approved $650,000 in Opportunities Fund support to invest in technical assistance and support for the groups at the core of the burgeoning #BlackLivesMatter movement.
>
> [...]
>
> That support calls into question how we might most appropriately support such efforts; specifically whether we should seek to shape the movement as opposed to facilitate its direct action. How do we confront the reality that such movements frequently flail as they attempt to grow and confront the challenges of institutionalizing themselves sufficiently to extend their reach? To what extent do we believe that we should play a role in helping such movement leaders connect with others that might help deepen policy recommendations or connections to sympathetic, but silent, inside actors? How can we help link such movements to existing grantees and other key actors that provide mutual strengthening? And throughout how do we make sure we follow the first rule of philanthropy in such circumstances, namely to do no harm? (In this vein, it is noteworthy how the Soros name is or can be used to try and delegitimize such movements).[14]

This passage gives direct insight into the mental gymnastics that members of the elite in our current political system must engage in to maintain their mental frame that they are not driving events. We have here the plain understanding that these protest-

licing. The Department of Justice recently selected the first six cities to host pilot sites for the National Initiative for Building Community Trust and Justice, which was launched last fall to help repair and strengthen the relationship between law enforcement and the communities they serve by exploring strategies intended to enhance procedural justice, reduce implicit bias, and support racial reconciliation." *Open Society U.S. Programs Board Meeting*, New York, May 7–8, 2015, 35, accessed June 4, 2019. https://s3.amazonaws.com/lifesite/-usp_may_2015_board_book.pdf.

14 *Open Society U.S. Programs Board Meeting*, New York, October 1–2, 2015, 22, accessed June 4, 2019. https://cdn.newsbusters.org/blog_attachment/-oct_2015_usp_board_book.pdf.

ing groups are unable to organise beyond very simple structures, and the recognition that they lack infrastructure, funds, and expertise. We also find the author struggling with the issue that funding and organisation by the elite is driving matters and shaping events, yet the author tries to maintain the conceit that this is mere facilitation of spontaneous and natural change. A further passage from the October 2015 Open Society Memo entitled "Black Lives Matter and the Challenges of Supporting Decentralized Movements"[15] is similarly confused, and again, reveals the institutional framework created by foundations in not just the Black Lives Matter movement, but also in immigration amnesty advocacy and the Occupy Wall Street movement. The total and utter dependency of these movements on foundation (and elite) structures and finance is, again, a source of serious anguish for the writer:

> The inherent tension between the organic nature of authentic movement-building and the need for institutional infrastructure has often stymied philanthropy in its efforts to effect social change. This begs the question of what is the appropriate role for philanthropy, in either supporting or defining policy agendas. Does philanthropy undermine the field when it advocates directly in spheres of political influence instead of empowering grantees to do the same? Are there times when philanthropy can use its levers of influence to expedite change as institutional actors mature?[16]

The self-deceit that this elite support is merely tilting the scales in the favour of a spontaneous and "organic" movement is clearly a key element in the mental gymnastics that a member of the elite must engage in within this dynamic.[17] The need of the elite to convince themselves that they are not really acting as the di-

---

15 *Open Society U.S. Programs Board Meeting*, New York, October 1–2, 2015, 21–23.

16 ibid., 21.

17 Consider also the recognition by Darren Walker that the Ford Foundation provided an infrastructure for civil rights. He is quoted as saying that the Ford Foundation is planning to create a "'social-justice infrastructure' reminiscent of the support it provided non-profits during the civil-rights era." Alex Daniels, "Ford Shifts Grant Making to Focus Entirely on Inequality," *The Chronicle of Philanthropy*, June 11, 2015. https://www.philanthropy.com/article/Ford-Shifts-Grant-Making-to/230839/.

rectors of this process has a psychologically strong pull on them, which can be seen in elite preference for theories of history of the Whiggish, Hegelian, or Marxist varieties. Such systems of thought provide a framework within which the actions of the elite can be reformulated in impersonal terms that provide a supposedly neutral point of rational agreement; the purpose of this being that their otherwise clearly conflict-driven actions become something other than resentment-fuelled attacks against other centres of power. The result is that the elite take on the mantle of the cause in a profound sense, and identify themselves as the underdog in a great struggle against an oppressive and evil superior force, despite being themselves in possession of superior resources. This oppressing force is, of course, identified as the much maligned right wing of the power structure, or, as we can describe it in Jouvenelian terms, the subsidiary structures of authority in the process of being undermined by the primary Power centre.

This curious underdog act is assisted by the inability of the right wing in modernity to understand or articulate what is happening. We can take, for example, the complaint raised by the author of the Open Society's memo that the actions of the foundation are often attacked by right wing references to George Soros' involvement. The unspoken implication of this complaint is that it is Soros' Jewish provenance which is at issue. Now, the right wing are not wrong in that Soros is heavily linked to left wing movements, and in that he is a guiding force by virtue of the funds he puts at the disposal of the various foundations that he administers; but what they miss, and where they veer into error, is that this involvement is not part of some coherent conspiracy, but is part of a far greater systemic issue.[18] A further look at other foundations acting in the same manner as Soros' Open Society Foundations provides added context. For example, the Ford Foundation, through the Borealis Philanthropy Organisation, is acting to provide the amount of $100 million to assist the movement, and they are not the only ones.[19] The one constant in all of

18 It is not the place of this work to offer a detailed analysis of the role of Jewish involvement in revolutionary movements and the effects that the Jouvenelian mechanism has had on the shaping of their culture. However, it is worth noting that, as outsiders, and, therefore, as members of the periphery, they form a section of the population that would naturally align with the centralising Power.
19 Valerie Richardson, "Black Lives Matter cashes in with $100 million

this is the support of federal governance and the elite in American society in a centralising manner, as dictated by their position within the Jouvenelian model—an elite which is self-effacing and acts through proxies, as predicted by Jouvenel.

A final, illuminating example of this thinking in practice is provided in another series of leaks that gives us unprecedented first-hand evidence of the interaction of societal elites: the John Podesta Wikileaks email leaks. John Podesta, the campaign manager for Hillary Clinton in the 2016 US election, is clearly part of the left wing, and in this series of e-mails we see exactly the same kind of thinking as that exhibited by the author of the Open Society memos. When writing of the undermining of the Catholic Church and the creation of a "Catholic Spring" in an email dated Feb 11th, 2012, 8:45 AM, Podesta writes the following:

> We created Catholics in Alliance for the Common Good to organize for a moment like this. But I think it lacks the leadership to do so now.
> Likewise Catholics United. Like most Spring movements, I think this one will have to be bottom up.[20]

Catholics in Alliance for the Common Good, and Catholics United, are non-profit organisations,[21] which are, therefore, supposedly part of a non-political private realm, but here we see Podesta clearly treating them as tools at his disposal with which to undermine enemy centres of power, here in the form of the Catholic Church. His deference to a "bottom up" movement is incongruous with the development of organisations which, he notes, "we created." The insistence on the spontaneity of a society which seems to always rise up against the elite's enemies is a central plank of power in the modern liberal structure.

Now we can turn our attention to the right wing, and we can see that, just as the left is the centralising elite of a power structure

---

from liberal foundations," *The Washington Post*, August 16, 2016. http://www.washingtontimes.com/news/2016/aug/16/black-lives-matter-cashes-100-million-liberal-foun/.

20　John Podesta, "Re: opening for a Catholic Spring? just musing…" email message to Sandy Newton and Tara McGuinness, February 11, 2012, accessed March 29, 2017. https://wikileaks.org/podesta-emails/emailid/57579.

21　Both organizations are, of course, funded by various philanthropic foundations.

acting in conjunction with a section of the periphery, the right is the remainder in this equation. The right wing is the agglomeration of actors who find themselves in that segment of the system which is impeding the centralising actions of the elite. This is the "reactionary" element which is responding to the "progressive" actions of the left in the act of centralisation. Just as with the left, the makeup of this right varies depending on location, time, and the nature of the conflicts and centralisation occurring within the given structure.

The history of conservatism is a testament to the ways in which the middle in this process is in a continual process of catching up to the developments created by centralisation. Fundamentally, conservatism is an amalgamation of positions and concepts which produce dissenting opinions that are acceptable to this primary Power structure, and are, as such, of no threat. Nowhere is this better demonstrated than in the sad image of Buckleyite conservatism with its intellectual vacuity that allowed for widespread acquiescence to the prevailing power structures that developed in the wake of WWII.

One of the more obvious criticisms of the model presented in this chapter is that changes in power structures occurred prior to those changes which marked the beginning of the left/right distinction. This would mean that we are possibly faced with the anachronistic task of claiming that left and right are universals of political structures. This is mistaken, since the development of a left and a right is a symptom of a fundamental and systematic blindness to the Jouvenelian mechanism which is fairly unique to modernity. The birth of these concepts is a result of the misunderstanding of the thinkers of modern democracy that they were not agents of centralisation, but that they were, instead, disinterested facilitators of a mass equality and individualism in the form of self-government. There is, however, a distinct continuation of the pattern of the employment of the periphery by kings, Popes, emperors, and, following the revolutions of the 17th and 18th centuries, by democratic governments that claimed that they did not really govern—but to claim that the kings were left wing makes little sense. Rather, it makes far greater sense to subsume both phenomena within the Jouvenelian model, and to maintain the Jouvenelian vocabulary. Doing so consigns the left/right distinction to the very specific governmental system within which it arose.

X

GEOPOLITICAL CONSIDERATIONS

THE role of geopolitical conflict in the development of the Jouvenelian model is significant, and we can divide this role into two broad categories: 1) the use of centralisation to increase the power of a given centre so as to make it better able to conduct war, and 2) the use of this process to undermine another foreign centre of Power so as to destabilise its order. With regard to the first category, one of the more pressing impetuses driving centralisation is the threat posed by geopolitical competitors. In a chapter of *On Power* entitled "Of Political Rivalry,"[1] Jouvenel provides a compelling argument that the push for centralisation by monarchs was rooted in the geopolitical environment within which they existed. It is the successful centralisation of one Power, and, consequently, its ability to utilise more internal resources, that forces other centres of Power to follow suit, as he writes: "war is like a sheepdog harrying laggard Powers to catch up their smarter fellows in the totalitarian race."[2] As such, Jouvenel makes the case that the initial success of the Spanish kingdom in centralising authority and raising taxes in the 17th century pushed both the French and English monarchies to follow suit and to proceed down the road to absolute monarchy. Jouvenel makes the interesting point that there is a notable correspondence in discontent over taxation in

1 Jouvenel, *On Power*, 135–156.
2 ibid., 142.

these three orders, which provides support for this claim.[3]

Another example provided by Jouvenel of the pressure to emulate centres of Power that had been more successful in centralisation is the *levée en masse* of Napoleon's armies. Other European nations had little option but to follow suit once the French had developed it, and, accordingly, they enacted conscription on a level that earlier kings could only have dreamed of. To this example we can also add that of the USA during the American Civil War. Here, the pressures created by conflict forced both sides, most notably the Confederacy, to engage in policies of centralisation. It was the Confederacy that introduced conscription on the North American continent with the Confederate Conscription Act of April 16th, 1862,[4] and this was followed by the Union with the Militia Act of July 17th, 1862, which also permitted the black population to serve. The Confederacy belatedly followed suit and instituted conscription of the black population shortly before the war's end.[5]

Whilst this process of centralisation and the undermining of subsidiaries can provide resources for a Power centre, it is open to the possibility of being subverted by another centre of Power and used against the initial beneficiary. The complexity of this dynamic can best be illustrated by analysing examples of this process in recent history, so that we can see how in one sphere this Jouvenelian promotion of the periphery can increase one primary Power's power, and in other instances, it can be a means of destabilisation. An instructive example for our purposes is supplied by the rise of Wahhabi Islam which has functioned as a tool for various power centres in various contexts.

It has become commonplace to compare modern developments in Islam, and the current turmoil of the Islamic world, to the Reformation, and such comparisons correctly note two similar

3 Jouvenel notes that the ship-money controversy, in which the English monarchy attempted to raise taxes unilaterally and found widespread resistance thereto, is dated to around 1637; the Revolt of the *va-nu-pieds* in Normandy, as a result of the French monarchy's attempt at taxation, occurred in 1639; and the Reapers' War (Catalonian Revolution), in response to the Spanish monarchy's attempt, occurred in 1640. In all cases, the cause was an attempt by the respective monarchies to increase taxation. Jouvenel, *On Power*, 146.
4 Emory M. Thomas, *The Confederacy as a Revolutionary Experience* (Columbia: University of South Carolina Press, 1991), 62.
5 ibid., 129–30.

symptoms of the same problem, but drastically mistake the underlying cause. As we have already covered in previous chapters, the Reformation was the result of Powers promoting an individualising and anti-tradition ontology, and in Wahhabism's success we see the same pattern of political conflict lurking beneath the surface. Like Protestantism, Wahhabism arose with the expansion and sponsorship of monarchical centres of Power—in this case, the house of Saud.[6] In many ways, the alliance formed between Muhammad ibn Abd al-Wahhab and Muhammad ibn Saud in 1744[7] represents an even clearer and more overt demonstration of the Jouvenelian model than does the development of Protestantism. Abd al-Wahhab actively sought out a patron in the form of first the ruler of Uyaynah—Uthmān ibn Muʿammar, a local rival of the Sauds—and then, when this proved abortive, he fled to Diriyah and sought out ibn Saud.[8] [9]

The value of Abd al-Wahhab and his Wahhabi doctrine to ibn Saud was that, as Madawi Al-Rasheed writes, "Wahhabism provided a novel impetus for political centralisation."[10] [11] Its many centralisation-friendly elements included not only demands of obedience to the emir as part of the duties of the believer, but also a tax called *zakat* payable to the emir, which was styled as an "Islamic tax to the leader of the Muslim community."[12] In addition, Wahhabism made it a duty of the believer to engage in *jihad* against non-believers and heretics under the guidance of the emir as the leader of the Islamic community of true believers. All of these developments allowed the emir to create a stable revenue stream with which to fund a standing army that

6 It should be noted that Muhammad ibn Abd al-Wahhab's first patron was not the House of Saud, but the ruler of Uyaynah, Uthmān ibn Muʿammar.

7 Wayne H. Bowen, *The History of Saudi Arabia* (Santa Barbara: Greenwood, 2008), 69.

8 Madawi Al-Rasheed, *A History of Saudi Arabia* (New York: Cambridge University Press, 2010), 15–16.

9 It appears that Muammar attempted to reverse his decision to expel al-Wahhab, and attempted, unsuccessfully, to encourage him to return—an example of patrons competing over systems of thought. Alexi Vassiliev, *The History of Saudi Arabia* (London: Saqi Books, 2000), 160.

10 Madawi Al-Rasheed, *A History of Saudi Arabia*, 17.

11 For an account of the centralising effects of this new and strictly monotheistic doctrine, see also Wayne H. Bowen, *The History of Saudi Arabia*, 72.

12 Madawi Al-Rasheed, *A History of Saudi Arabia*, 15.

was loyal, dependent on him, and driven by Islamic belief in the justification of aggression against the emir's enemies. As for the governance of the territory under his control, the Wahhabi *ulama* who preached the doctrines of Wahhabism formed the backbone of an infrastructure which was, again, dependent on the emir. This infrastructure allowed him to begin breaking down the localised relationships in the region that impeded these centralising attempts.[13] This resulted in the creation of the first Saudi kingdom, the Emirate of Diriyah from 1744 to 1818, which was ended with military force by the Ottoman Empire with the conclusion of the Wahhabi War of 1811–1818. There was to be a second expansion of the House of Saud between 1824 and 1891 (the Emirate of Nejd), but this also failed to last due to military setbacks, and, as a result, the Sauds were expelled following the Battle of Mulayda.

With the entry of the Ottoman Empire into WWI, we find the third and final emergence of a Saudi State, this time sponsored and protected by the British Empire. By setting themselves against the interests of the British Empire with their entrance into the war on the side of Germany, the Ottoman rulers encouraged a British policy of supporting proxies on the Ottoman periphery to divert and divide their military resources, beneficiaries of which policy included the House of Saud.[14] Another apparent factor in British support for this periphery was the worry that the Ottoman sultan would call a holy war so as to encourage unrest in territories held by the allied Powers that had substantial Muslim populations. Such a *fatwa* was actually issued in the name of Sultan Mehmed V in November 1914, but it had little effect, and was not supported by the emir of Mecca, Sarif Husain, who sided with the British Empire, and formed the focal point of a British funded and supplied Arab revolt.[15] Despite the initial favour enjoyed by Husain, the ultimate benefactor of this British support on the peninsula would turn out to be the House of Saud, despite the Sauds proving of little assistance against the Ottomans. Ibn Saud received subsidies past the end of the war, with these sub-

13 Wayne H. Bowen, *The History of Saudi Arabia*, 71.
14 Most of the details of this narrative are provided in Mark Curtis, *Secret Affairs: Britain's Collusion with Radical Islam* (London: Serpents Tail, 2018).
15 See Gary Troeller, "Anglo-Saudi Relations during the First World War," in *The Birth of Saudi Arabia: Britain and the Rise of the House of Saud* (London: Routledge, 2013), 73–126.

sidies only being discontinued on March 21st, 1923, as a result of British dissatisfaction with the increasing menace posed by his *Ikhwan* force,[16] a military contingent created so that the House of Saud would have a reliable and loyal fighting force independent of the subsidiaries of the Saudi order.[17] It was this *Ikhwan* force which allowed the House of Saud to defeat Sarif Husain and capture Mecca. The resulting fait accompli of Saudi dominance over the peninsula was accepted by British authorities, but as soon as the *Ikhwan* began to operate on their own imperative and turned towards attacking territories of interest to the British Empire, they fell afoul of both the House of Saud and the British Empire. At this point, this force for centralisation turned into a force opposed to centralisation, and its leaders began plotting to dispose of the House of Saud and to divide up the captured territories among themselves.[18] As a result, the *Ikhwan* came under attack by not only the House of Saud—still supplied by the British Empire[19]—but also by the Royal Air Force and British ground forces. The *Ikhwan*'s continued attacks on British protectorates had proved to be a fatal mistake, and British intervention proved decisive.

The British and Saudi alliance with Wahhabism, however, did not end with the *Ikhwan*, but continued via thinkers who were less extreme and more amenable to the House of Saud—a feat made possible by the simple expediency of controlling the funding and institutions that provided the structure for these cultural developments. The variants of Wahhabism that were supportive of the prevailing authorities remained institutionalised; those variants that were not were ended or made irrelevant.

Following WWII, British suzerainty was replaced by American, and the region took on a new importance due to the new strategic importance of its oil supplies. The Saudi State, far from being some ancient and backward one, is a very modern develop-

---

16 Troeller, *The Birth of Saudi Arabia*, 193.

17 For a full account of the role of the *Ikhwan* in the centralisation of the Saudi order, see Vassiliev, "Increased Centralization and the *Ikhwani* Movement (1926–1934)," in *The History of Saudi Arabia*, 544–84.

18 Vassiliev, *The History of Saudi Arabia*, 563.

19 While the *Ikhwan*, who were supposedly under the control of the Saudis, were attacking British protectorates, Britain was supplying the Saudis with munitions. ibid., 561.

ment, and owes its successful centralisation to the ability of the House of Saud to overcome its dependency on the tribal structures under its control, accomplished with the assistance of Britain, and later, of America. Following the success of Saudi consolidation of power, further geopolitical flashpoints created an even greater impetus for the spread of Wahhabi-style Islamic movements. Key to our understanding of the role of Islam in the present world is to understand the situation that existed between the USSR and the American-led International Community during the Cold War, a period which would prove formative for many cultural trends that we shall cover shortly. Two of the more significant focal points for the development of modern Islam are presented in the creation of Pakistan in 1947, and the Soviet–Afghan War of 1979–89.

With the partition of British India into India and Pakistan, General Zia-ul-Haq, president of Pakistan, utilised Wahhabi as well as Deobandi Islamic schools of thought[20] as a means to consolidate a new country, and to undermine secessionist movements in a manner echoing the actions of the House of Saud in the 18th, 19th, and early 20th centuries. This was done with the help of Saudi financing, as the oil wealth of Saudi Arabia had become a major geostrategic weapon in the hands (by proxy) of the Western powers. Not only was this Islamic faith advanced by Zia to support his own rule, but it was then exported at the expense of Afghanistan's Marxist government through the development of a string of *madrassas* along the Pakistan–Afghan border. These schools of thought were not spontaneous or organic, but were supported by General Zia and a cross-network of funds from the Saudi General Intelligence Department (GID), as well as by charities funded by wealthy Saudi patrons in line with formal Saudi funding. As Stephen Coll notes in *Ghost Wars*:

> Zia strongly encouraged personal religious piety within the Pakistan army's officer corps, a major change from the past. He encouraged the financing and construction of hundreds of *madrassas* or religious schools, along the Afghan frontier.[21]

20   For a brief overview of the history of Deobandi Islam and its connection to Pakistan, see Luv Puri, "The Past and Future of Deobandi Islam," *CTC Sentinel*, Vol. 2, Issue 11, (November 2009): 19–22, https://ctc.usma.edu/.

21   Steve Coll, *Ghost Wars: The Secret History of the CIA, Afghanistan, and bin Laden, from the Soviet Invasion to September 10, 2001* (London: Penguin Books, 2005),

An eye-opening statistic is also provided by Coll, "[i]n 1971 there had been only nine hundred madrassas in all of Pakistan. By the summer of 1988 there were about eight thousand official religious schools and an estimated twenty-five thousand unregistered ones."[22] The role of Power here is clear.

As we would expect from the Jouvenelian angle, Coll makes it clear that the incentives Zia had for supporting Islamism at the expense of other power centres were numerous. Pakistan, for a start, is a country comprised of a number of ethnic groups, and Pashtun nationalism, in particular, was a concern; hence, Coll reports that the CIA's station chief in Islamabad, Howard Hart, was of the opinion that Pakistan's Inter-Services Intelligence (ISI) favoured Muslim Brotherhood linked groups in Afghanistan because it weakened groups "likely to stir up Pashtun nationalism inside Pakistani territory."[23] This policy of favouring Islamic groups acting as competitors for secular movements that were threatening to certain power centres would be repeated many times in the Middle East. One clear example of this is provided by Israel's support of Hamas (Islamists) as a means to weaken the Palestinian Liberation Organisation (PLO) (secular socialists).[24]

Having spread Wahhabi-style Islam throughout Pakistan, the arrival of the Soviet–Afghan War would prove to be the next geopolitical breeding ground, as the United States, Pakistan, and Saudi Arabia used Islamic groups to act as proxies in conflict with the Soviet forces that had entered Afghanistan in support of the Afghan government. Saudi influence in the conflict resulted from geopolitical concern over the strategic importance of Afghanistan, and over the potential threat posed by the USSR if it gained a strong foothold there—a concern shared by the USA and Pakistan. This prompted a joint effort by both the USA and the Saudis to fund the Afghan conflict via the additional proxy of Pakistan's ISI, which was itself acting covertly in supplying the Afghan rebels. The Saudis even agreed to match US funding dollar for dollar. It is clear that without these funds, prolonged conflict in Afghanistan and successful resistance to Soviet intervention would have

61.

22 Coll, *Ghost Wars*, 180.

23 ibid., 68.

24 Andrew Higgins, "How Israel Helped to Spawn Hamas," *The Wall Street Journal,* January 24, 2009. https://www.wsj.com/articles/SB123275572295011847.

been inconceivable, and this funding reached astonishing levels before the war ended. Following the initial success of the Afghan War in causing serious problems for the Soviets, US funding reached $470 million in 1986 ($1.09 billion in adjusted 2019 dollars), and $630 million in 1987 ($1.4 billion in adjusted 2019 dollars). Each figure was, again, matched by Saudi's GID, and then augmented by donations from informal Saudi channels.[25]

So, we can see quite clearly that the success and development of Wahhabi Islam, as with Protestantism, owes little to any sort of dialectical development of concepts in accordance with reason, but, instead, was merely the by-product of the sustained and brutal geopolitical conflict to which it lent significant assistance, either as a means of centralisation, or as a means of destabilisation of enemy orders. US assistance in the process is especially egregious given the consequences of this development, as we saw with the 9/11 attacks. Attempts at expanding the conflict into Central Asia were apparently authorised by CIA head William Casey, with Afghan rebels carrying CIA-printed Holy Korans in the Uzbek language[26] entering Uzbekistan using CIA-provided weaponry. It appears to have been very clear US policy to encourage the spread of Islam against Soviet governance. That these strict adherents of Islam would have trouble differentiating modern Western states from Soviet states, and would then direct their attention to America, was not deeply considered by Western analysts.

With the fall of the USSR, Western and Gulf support for Wahhabi Islam as a military geopolitical tool has continued. Take the case of the recent Syrian conflict. It is not particularly important for us to speculate on specifically why Western and Gulf states have taken a keen interest in deposing Bashar al-Assad's government, because it would distract us from the far more important point that in taking this course of action they have observably supported Wahhabists. A declassified US Defense Intelligence Agency (DIA) document reveals that Western and Gulf state support of Islamists is a given fact, as it notes:

B, The Salafist, the Muslim Brotherhood, and AQI are the

---

25 Coll, *Ghost Wars*, 151.
26 ibid., 104.

major forces driving the insurgency in Syria.

C, The West, Gulf countries, and Turkey support the opposition, while Russia, China and Iran support the regime.[27]

The Syrian conflict mirrors the Afghan conflict to such a degree that we even see the same dynamic of multiple revenue streams operating concurrently from the Gulf States and the West. In a speech addressed to Goldman Sachs, then Secretary of State Clinton made the following remarks in relation to the US weapons transfers to Syria:

> "Some of us thought, perhaps, we could, with a more robust, covert action trying to vet, identify, train and arm cadres of rebels that would at least have the firepower to be able to protect themselves against both Assad and the Al-Qaeda-related jihadist groups that have, unfortunately, been attracted to Syria," she noted. "That's been complicated by the fact that the Saudis and others are shipping large amounts of weapons—and pretty indiscriminately—not at all targeted toward the people that we think would be the more moderate, least likely, to cause problems in the future, but this is another one of those very tough analytical problems."[28]

One can only wonder if the US dollar for dollar agreement has been replicated between the GID and US institutions.

The revelation of Western actors supporting political Islam for geopolitical purposes provides insight into the seeming incompetence of security agencies surrounding the free movement of so-called Islamic extremists in the West. One particularly pertinent example of this link between British security agencies and these radicals is provided by the example of Abu Muntasir who was allowed free rein within the United Kingdom by security services:

> Muntasir, who is seen sobbing in the film as he recounts the

27 Judicial Watch, *Department of Defense Information Report*, 14-L-0552/DIA/ 289, accessed March 3, 2017. http://www.judicialwatch.org/wp-content/uploads/2015/05/Pg.-291-Pgs.-287-293-JW-v-DOD-and-State-14-812-DOD-Release-2015-04-10-final-version11.pdf.

28 Zaid Jilani, "In Secret Goldman Sachs Speech, Hillary Clinton Admitted No-Fly Zone Would 'Kill a Lot of Syrians,'" *The Intercept*, October 10, 2016. https://theintercept.com/2016/10/10/in-secret-goldman-sachs-speech-hillary-clinton-admitted-no-fly-zone-would-kill-a-lot-of-syrians/.

horrors of his own days on battlefields in Bosnia, Afghanistan and Burma, is described as one of the "founding fathers of western jihad" and admitted that he worked to "create the link and clear the paths. I came back [from war] and opened the door and the trickle turned to a flood. I inspired and recruited, I raised funds and bought weapons, not just a one-off but for 15 to 20 years. Why I have never been arrested I don't know."[29]

We do not have to be as confused as Muntasir. Islamic violence is, in actuality, a valuable resource to elements of Western liberal governments; a resource which, in response to its blowback on the Western world in the form of terrorist attacks, results in the need for management by these same elements.[30] Not only is there clear support from foreign policy officials seeking to use these Islamists as a fighting force for geopolitical conflict, but there is the added complexity created by the electoral value of these Muslim populations to centralising elites. It is often the case that these Muslim populations, as with all minority populations, can be relied upon to support globalist elites in an unspoken alliance against opponents of centralisation. The rapid rise of Islamic populations in Europe—from practically non-existence in the 1950s to close to 10% of many Western states' populations (and still increasing drastically)—has resulted in a situation in which the governing elite, acting in a purely Jouvenelian manner, are electorally aligning with this immigrant population against the native population. The increase of this section of the population is, therefore, of great systemic interest to the progressive elite, and any negative response will be met with creative means to undermine that re-

29 Tracy McVeigh, "'Recruiter' of UK jihadis: 'I regret opening the way to Isis'," *The Guardian*, June 13, 2015. https://www.theguardian.com/world/2015/jun/13/godfather-of-british-jihadists-admits-we-opened-to-way-to-join-isis.
30 There are clear indications that in the wake of terrorist attacks, elements of Western governments and security services have taken to instigating and directing supposedly spontaneous outpourings of grief and solidarity. This includes the apparently organised creation and dissemination of posters, hashtags, flowers at the site of the attack, as well as the organisation of mass gatherings of Imams denouncing terror attacks and the development of "grassroots" anti-extremist groups and movements. See Ian Cobain, "'Mind control': The secret UK government blueprints shaping post-terror planning," *Middle East Eye*, May 22, 2019. https://www.middleeasteye.net/news/mind-control-secret-british-government-blueprints-shaping-post-terror-planning.

sponse. The development of such neologisms as "Islamophobia" is an excellent example of this, with its attempt at abusively consigning any objection to this demographic development to mental illness.

It should be noted, however, that within the Arab world Islamic violence seems to be a secondary option at best, and if camera-friendly, progressive Muslims can be found to serve the same purpose, they will be; however, they have historically lacked the staying power of Islamic radicals, and so have been selected out by geopolitical exigency. We can see this when we widen our scope to look at the wave of protests that sparked the Arab Spring, and we are faced with the by-now-familiar spectacle of "top down" grassroots movements.

Our first clue as to what happened in the Arab Spring is found in an article in the New York Times entitled *U.S. Groups Helped Nurture Arab Uprisings*. The story presented by the author is predictable in that it makes it clear that the movement was brought into being for geopolitical purposes by US institutions, as it notes, inadvertently, by revealing that:

> …key leaders of the movements having been trained by the Americans in campaigning, organizing through new media tools and monitoring elections.[31]

This would seem to indicate that US officials and elements of the Power structure engaged in the organisation, training, and funding of proxy actors agitating for equality and liberty to undermine other power centres, which is confirmed from the wealth of cable leaks by WikiLeaks,[32] as well as by numerous candid newspaper

---

31 Ron Nixon, "U.S. Groups Helped Nurture Arab Uprisings," *The New York Times*, April 14, 2011. http://www.nytimes.com/2011/04/15/world/15aid.html?_r=3&pagewanted=1&emc=eta1.

32 For example, see the cables relating to the US embassy in Egypt and their support of Egyptian protestors. Embassy Egypt, "APRIL 6 ACTIVIST ON HIS U.S. VISIT AND REGIME CHANGE IN EGYPT," WikiLeaks Cable: 08CAIRO2572_a, dated December 30, 2008. https://wikileaks.org/plusd/cables/08CAIRO2572_a.html; Embassy Egypt, "APRIL 6 ACTIVIST DESCRIBES GOE HARASSMENT, REQUESTS INFORMATION ON YOUTH MOVEMENTS SUMMIT," WikiLeaks Cable: 08CAIRO2431_a, dated November 26, 2008. https://wikileaks.org/plusd/cables/08CAIRO2431_a.html.

articles such as the New York Times articles entitled *Shy U.S. Intellectual Created Playbook Used in Revolution*,[33] and *A Tunisian-Egyptian Link That Shook Arab History*.[34] The articles outline a narrative in which the International Center on Nonviolent Conflict ran workshops to train demonstrators in both Tunisia and Egypt on how to undermine "police states," provided organisational advice, fostered connections, provided funds, etc. The organised nature of the protests is highlighted by the wonderfully unreflective quote by one Mr. Ghonim that he had "never seen a revolution that was preannounced before."[35]

Turning our attention now to the Tunisian arm of the Arab Spring, we can approach with a great deal of scepticism the accepted narrative that the cause of the unrest was the self-immolation of a street trader in Sidi Bouzid.[36] It is noteworthy that there had been previous examples of self-immolation, as well as many protests that did not lead to nationwide revolt, so an explanation as to why this one did so must be advanced. In supplying just such an explanation, we can first look for an actor promoting and organising the protests in a way that did not exist before. This actor was the Sidi Bouzid branch of the General Union of Tunisian Workers (UGTT), as revealed by an Al Jazeera article entitled *How Tunisia's Revolution Began*:

> The protests that erupted in Sidi Bouzid were indeed spontaneous, yet they were marked by a level of organisation and sophistication that appears grounded in the sheer determination of those who participated in them.
>
> The Sidi Bouzid branch of the UGTT was engaged in the uprising from day one.
>
> While the national leadership of the Tunisian General Labour Union (UGTT) is generally viewed as lacking po-

33 Sheryl Gay Stolberg, "Shy U.S. Intellectual Created Playbook Used in a Revolution," *The New York Times*, February 16, 2011. https://www.nytimes.com/2011/02/17/world/middleeast/17sharp.html.

34 David D. Kirkpatrick and David E. Sanger, "A Tunisian-Egyptian Link That Shook Arab History," *The New York Times*, February 13, 2011. http://www.nytimes.com/2011/02/14/world/middleeast/14egypt-tunisia-protests.html?pagewanted=all&_r=0.

35 ibid.

36 See the article by Robert F. Worth, "How a Single Match Can Ignite a Revolution," *The New York Times*, January 21, 2011. https://www.nytimes.com/2011/01/23/weekinreview/23worth.html.

litical independence from the ruling class, its regional representatives have a reputation for gutsy engagement.

"The major driving force behind these protesters is the
Sidi Bouzid union, which is very strong," said Affi Fethi,
who teaches physics at a local high school.[37]

This role played by UGTT is, again, not a random occurrence,
but is in line with details outlined in a cable dated February 22nd,
2007. The cable in question summarises a call between the US
ambassador and the UGTT Secretary General. The UGTT is
described as "a natural ally on our Freedom Agenda goals."[38] [39]
The cable then goes on to record the UGTT Secretary General
claiming that:

> ...the American people and government historically were
> respected internationally for supporting peace, democra-
> cy, human rights and freedom. Tunisians today still believe
> these are shared Tunisian-American values[40]

So we see a warm relationship between the UGTT and the US,
which includes increased co-operation and funding from the US,
as the cable concludes, "Post will follow up with Jerad to encourage greater cooperation, including through MEPI funding and
PD programs."[41] "MEPI" is seemingly a reference to the Middle
East Partnership Initiative run by the State Department, with
"PD" presumably being a reference to participatory development
programs. We see very clearly from primary sources that the US
spent considerable time increasing the resources and competency
of opponents of the Tunisian government. This increasing support

37 Yasmine Ryan, "How Tunisia's revolution began," *Al Jazeera*, January 26, 2011.
http://www.aljazeera.com/indepth/features/2011/01/2011126121815985483.
html.
38 Embassy Tunisia, "UNION LEADER HIGHLIGHTS SHARED VAL-
UES, DISILLUSION WITH US POLICY," WikiLeaks Cable: 07TUNIS246_a,
dated February 22, 2007. https://wikileaks.org/plusd/cables/07TUNIS246_a.
html.
39 For an overview of the Bush administration's Freedom Agenda, see "Freedom
Agenda," Policies in Focus, President George W. Bush Archives, accessed March
3, 2019. https://georgewbush-whitehouse.archives.gov/infocus/freedomagenda/.
40 Embassy Tunisia, "UNION LEADER HIGHLIGHTS SHARED
VALUES," WikiLeaks Cable: 07TUNIS246_a. https://wikileaks.org/plusd/
cables/07TUNIS246_a.html.
41 ibid.

for activists is covered in *Tunisia: From Stability to Revolution in the Maghreb* where the author claims:

> Particularly after the 11 September attacks, the US government became concerned that Ben Ali's sclerotic kleptocracy could become a liability rather than an asset. The embassy in Tunis became critical of Ben Ali and increased contact with opposition organizations.[42]

This is augmented by the claim that "opposition activists also believed that Ben Ali's grip was slipping and that powerful international actors had lost some of their confidence in him,"[43] and that "[a] range of legal and illegal opposition parties and civil society organizations had become more active and begun to cooperate with one another."[44]

This narrative matches the cables. The US began providing funds, organising the opposition, and laying the groundwork for the overthrow of the government for some time beforehand. Further diplomatic cables from the US Tunisian embassy only support this. One cable entitled "What should we do?" is quite strange in that it lays out a picture of the Tunisian GOT as a benign regime with the foreign policy goal of simply "to get along with everyone [sic],"[45] yet the cable displays a perplexing anger from the embassy over vague human rights complaints and over having their movements curtailed so that they struggled:

> ...to maintain contact with a wide swath of Tunisian society. GOT-controlled newspapers often attack Tunisian civil society activists who participate in Embassy activities, portraying them as traitors.[46]

This contact was needed because the US supposedly has, "an interest in fostering greater political openness and respect for hu-

42 Christopher Alexander, *Tunisia: From Stability to Revolution in the Maghreb* (New York: Routledge, 2016), 74.
43 ibid.,75.
44 ibid.,77.
45 Embassy Tunisia, "TROUBLED TUNISIA: WHAT SHOULD WE DO?" WikiLeaks Cable: 09TUNIS492_a, dated July 17, 2009. https://search.wikileaks.org/plusd/cables/09TUNIS492_a.html.
46 ibid.

man rights."[47] The cable advises that the US should change its approach to one where:

> The key element is more and frequent high-level private candor. We recommend being explicit with GOT leaders that we are changing our approach, while also making clear that we will continue to engage privately with opposition parties and civil society.[48]

This increased communication is outlined in the following relevant section:

> In addition to talking to the GOT, we need to engage directly with the Tunisian people, especially youth. The Embassy is already using Facebook as a communication tool. In addition, we have the Ambassador's blog, a relatively new undertaking that is attracting attention. Over the past couple of years, the Embassy has substantially increased its outreach to Tunisian youth through concerts, film festivals, and other events. Our information resource center and America's Corners are popular ways for Tunisians to access unfiltered news and information. We should continue and increase such programs.[49]

The Tunisian government, then, seems to have been guilty of doing no more than asserting its authority to determine cultural developments within its territory. The US actors, meanwhile, are clearly acting as predatory and aggressive entities.

The clear involvement of US officials on numerous levels in the Tunisian Revolution is also demonstrated by further WikiLeaks cables. One leak, dated January 23rd, 2007, details a roundtable discussion between NEA Deputy Assistant Secretary, J. Scott Carpenter, and six "prominent members of Tunisian civil society" to discuss democracy advocacy support.[50] More context is provid-

---

47   Embassy Tunisia, "TROUBLED TUNISIA," WikiLeaks Cable: 09TUNIS492_a.   https://search.wikileaks.org/plusd/cables/09TUNIS492_a. html.
48   ibid.
49   ibid.
50   Embassy Tunisia, "DAS CARPENTER'S ROUNDTABLE WITH TUNISIAN CIVIL SOCIETY," WikiLeaks Cable: 07TUNIS102_a, dated January 23, 2007. https://wikileaks.org/plusd/cables/07TUNIS102_a.html.

ed in a further cable on democratisation of the region in which it is recorded that then Secretary of State Clinton:

> ...emphasized the importance of civil society's role in the G8-BMENA Forum for the Future process. She highlighted the role youth play in the region; noted the use of technology as an important tool to reach young audiences; and said the USG wants to provide technological support to civil society. Civil society representatives expressed tremendous and heartfelt gratitude to the Secretary for her support for the Forum for the Future. Participants also expressed the need for continued USG support for civil society initiatives in the region, and stressed that the USG should not ignore issues such as human rights and democracy when engaging with governments in the region.[51]

This reference to technology is key to the question of why the Arab Spring occurred when it did. The key to this puzzle lies in the lines of communication open to the orders in question. It is fairly well known that in Tunisia, media had been largely monopolised by the government, as mentioned in previously cited cables. To get around this monopoly, social media was utilised. In particular, Facebook and Twitter provided means for organisation, something we have seen yet again more recently with US officials requesting that Twitter help Iranian protestors.[52] Another pertinent example is that of the US security establishment's attempts at creating a Cuban social media network, ZunZuneo, to help overthrow the Cuban government.[53] The US fostered, organised, and funded social unrest, with the overall aim of removing disfavoured regimes by using platforms for organisation that the regimes in question could not control. Of course, the elements of the US Power structure then worked very diligently to efface their role, and the revolution then became a "force of nature," or "the

---

51 Embassy Morocco, "SECRETARY CHALLENGES BMENA CIVIL SOCIETY," WikiLeaks Cable: 09RABAT921_a, dated November 22, 2009. https://wikileaks.org/plusd/cables/09RABAT921_a.html.
52 Ewan MacAskill, "US confirms it asked Twitter to stay open to help Iran protesters," *The Guardian*, June 17, 2009. https://www.theguardian.com/world/2009/jun/17/obama-iran-twitter.
53 Associated Press in Washington, "US secretly created 'Cuban Twitter' to stir unrest and undermine government," *The Guardian*, April 3, 2014. https://www.theguardian.com/world/2014/apr/03/us-cuban-twitter-zunzuneo-stir-unrest.

will of a collection of self-sovereign individuals comprising the people," as opposed to the predatory actions of a foreign Power centre enforcing change by means considered illegitimate according to its own rules of engagement.[54] Of course, it is not only the Muslim world which has been subject to great cultural upheaval as a result of geopolitical conflict and the utilisation of peripheries, but also the Western world, and it is to this that we can now turn, as these changes have, if anything, been even more badly misinterpreted by political theorists.

---

54 It is somewhat ironic that the election of Donald Trump was facilitated by the very same social media, and has undermined many of the same progressive sections of Power which had so eagerly utilised this means against other regions.

XI

THE INTERNATIONAL COMMUNITY

Like Central Asia and the Middle East in our current time, following the end of WWII, Western Europe was a particularly important geopolitical focal point, with British and American control over their respective spheres of influence made precarious by the imposition of parliamentary democracies. Communist parties in many of these democracies enjoyed a great deal of popularity, and to counter this, various techniques were employed by the Western Powers to ensure that elections went in a satisfactory direction. To understand how seriously this threat of communist electoral success was taken, we have only to turn our attention to the Gladio "stay-behind" network and the political destabilisation which it fomented in countries such as Italy in a bid to discredit these popular communist parties.[1]

In 1946, partisan networks were created with the express aim of forming a ready-made resistance in the event of a Soviet land invasion of Western Europe. Many of the men recruited were members of the previous fascist or Nazi infrastructures of Germany and Italy, or other right wing groups with a reliably anti-communist stance. These networks were supplied with weapons, training, and money by the British MI6 and the American

---

1 For an in-depth investigation into the actions of this network, see Daniele Ganser, *NATO's Secret Armies: Operation GLADIO and Terrorism in Western Europe* (London: Frank Cass, 2005).

Office for Strategic Services (OSS), later to be replaced by the CIA. This network became known as Gladio, and its existence was acknowledged after many years of secrecy when Giulio Andreotti, the Italian Prime Minister, revealed it in a speech to the Italian Parliament on October 24th, 1990.[2] While this group was supposed to act as a stay-behind fighting force in the event of a war which never came, it was, instead, pressed into use for more immediate needs. Specifically, there is evidence, and even acknowledgment from security services, that these networks were used to manipulate public opinion against communist parties and factions by committing false flag terror attacks. The method of these false flags was for a Gladio group, using Gladio weaponry, to commit some form of atrocity in a way that made it appear to be committed by communist agents.

In such an environment, one where committing false flag terrorism is deemed acceptable, conscious, widespread involvement in all areas of culture must surely have seemed a logical and minor step in ensuring electoral control. It is, therefore, unsurprising that we find in this conflict the widespread, acknowledged involvement of US institutions in every area of Western European culture. A perfect example of this involvement can be found in the Congress for Cultural Freedom, a CIA creation which was used to fund vast numbers of artistic and literary events and publications. Following a revelation by *The New York Times* that this funding came from the CIA, the organisation was renamed the International Association for Cultural Freedom (IACF), and the funding burden was taken up by the all-too-familiar Ford Foundation.[3] This pattern of the same elite funding developments through either formal (yet secret) avenues like government agencies, or through informal "private" entities, is very helpful in disguising what is, in fact, the same elite cast of characters in either case. Despite this particular organisation proving abortive, there is a strong case to be made that any thinker or artist of renown in this post-war period, and any movement of significance in gener-

2   Clare Pedrick, "CIA ORGANIZED SECRET ARMY IN WESTERN EUROPE," *The Washington Post*, November 14, 1990. https://www.washingtonpost.com/archive/politics/1990/11/14/cia-organized-secret-army-in-western-europe/e0305101-97b9-4494-bc18-d89f42497d85/?utm_term=.a2c2f1b2ff63.
3   See Frances Stonor Saunders, *The Cultural Cold War: The CIA and the World of Arts and Letters* (New York: New Press, 2000), 411–13.

al, was ultimately patronised by the US elite nexus of intelligence services or foundations, often both at once.

What is of special interest to us regarding this cultural clash between the Soviets and the International Community (as this Anglo-American dominated sphere came to be called) is the nature of the cultural developments that it incentivised. The Jouvenelian model tells us that this conflict should follow a pattern wherein we can see appeals to the periphery made through calls to equality and/or individuality as a means to undermine competing centres of power, and here we find this in abundance. Consider the following from a CIA draft study regarding its involvement in the aforementioned Congress for Cultural Freedom:

> [T]his organization of scholars and artists—egotistical, free-thinking, and even anti-American in their politics—managed to reach out from its Paris headquarters to demonstrate that Communism, despite its blandishments, was a deadly foe of art and thought.[4]

Note that the author recognises that the focus was on freedom and liberty—or rather, on an American interpretation of freedom and liberty—as against the so-called communist "blandishments." Also, note that the US patrons were obviously more than happy to fund artists and thinkers who were in a sense anti-American, as long as they were anti-communist. This was far less dangerous than it may sound, since even if this anti-Americanism became a problem, the patrons would be able to simply withdraw funding. Without funding for study, books, finance for attending conferences, and all the other logistical requirements for cultural prominence, these artists would, and did, slide into obscurity.

This Anglo-American institutional control of culture in the newly christened International Community clearly bears all the hallmarks of the Jouvenelian model, with its appeals to freedom and liberty in a self-effacing process. Two of the more influential developments in this regard deserve singling out as especially Jouvenelian in their development, and these are the now ubiquitous

---

4 Central Intelligence Agency, *Studies in Intelligence: Origins of the Congress for Cultural Freedom, 1949–50*. Declassified draft study. Date unknown. https://web.archive.org/web/20060616213245/http://cia.gov/csi/studies/95unclass/Warner.html.

feminism and anti-racism. To see how utterly dependent these individualising and equalising concepts were on this patronage and the geopolitical pressures of the time, we can, again, return to the Google Ngram tool, and look at the historical frequency of the terms "feminism" and "racism" (Fig. 1). In doing so, what we see is exactly what we would expect to see, given the centrality of patronage and geopolitical conflict.

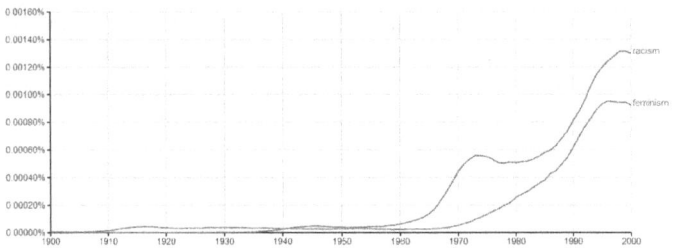

Figure 1. Frequency of the terms *racism* and *feminism* found in Google's text corpora.

The reader will note the clear uptick for both concepts in the 1960s and 1970s during the height of the CIA's and various foundations' promotion of both of these concepts. The patron and his money are always determinative of what culture flourishes, and this is the same for Islamism in Afghanistan during the Soviet–Afghan War and feminism and anti-racism in Western Europe in the Cold War period.

With feminism, it appears that Soviet calls for the equality of women in the post-war period were met with consternation by Anglo-American elites. These elites, therefore, appear to have determined that they would need to create competing institutions to press the Western claim that liberalism (Western-aligned governance), and not communism (Soviet-aligned governance), was the most beneficial system for female emancipation, and it was from these institutions that feminism, in its current guise, developed. To this end, not only were CIA funds employed in the creation of such organisations as the Committee for Correspondence,[5] but so too were foundation funds controlled by the same

5 The name chosen for this organisation specifically references the American War of Independence as this was the name of the organisations set up in the various colonies that organised the rebellion.

elite. As with the Congress for Cultural Freedom, the CIA funding of the Committee for Correspondence was uncovered and revealed by the American media in 1967, and again, the funding for feminism fell to the foundations.

One key driver for this focus on the claims of women's liberty is linked to the increasing social importance of women resulting from electoral politics. The interaction between the competing American and Soviet claims to female empowerment resulted in the liberal camp stressing the spontaneous individual to a far greater degree than the Soviet side which, by all accounts, focused on a far more honest feminist theory based on overt state-led emancipation. The key to the liberal position's success was the presentation of their feminism as a grassroots development, as against the relatively clumsy Soviet state-led version, because this allowed Western structures of authority to operate with relative impunity, and, therefore, with more effectiveness.[6] As we can again note, this focus on the grassroots claim hid the true extent of institutional involvement, something we see when we consider the UN's Fourth World Conference on Women in 1985 where the Ford Foundation had become so involved that they had spent nearly $5 million ($11.8 million in adjusted 2019 dollars).[7] The impact of this on this movement was decisive, and we can see this in a quote from the feminist Susan Berresford:

> Speaking about the women's rights leaders, who were, she said, "wonderful people," Berresford speculated, "I think they would have had their voices heard anyway." But then frankness entered into her comments: "But I think it made a difference that there was a funder ready to back them. And we stuck with the [women's] organizations and people for a long time."[8]

---

6   For an account of the conflict between these two variants of feminism, see Chiara Bonfiglioli, "The First UN World Conference on Women (1975) as a Cold War Encounter: Recovering Anti-Imperialist, Non-Aligned and Socialist Genealogies," in *Filozofija i drustvo*, 27(3) (January 2016): 521–41, https://doi.org/10.2298/FID1603521B.

7   This does not take into account the additional funding provided by other foundations, such as the Carnegie Corporation. Korey, *Taking on the World's Repressive Regimes*, 242–43.

8   ibid., 245.

A similar dynamic to what we see here at work with feminism was also in play with the development of modern anti-racism.

The reader may recall from chapter 9 that, in our review of civil rights, we noted that there was a curious tendency for civil rights to be connected with matters of geopolitical concern. The example of the friend of the court brief found in the Brown v. Board of Education of Topeka 1954 case is symptomatic of this, as here we find federal representatives citing foreign affairs in a matter to which it would seem to have little relevance. This intervention by the Justice Department at the instigation of the Truman presidency is part of a larger pattern of behaviour by this same federally aligned elite in the mid-20th century, in which, along with a vast increase in US military presence and intervention in the wider world, there is a concomitant move towards racial equality within the US and other aligned Western states themselves. These two developments are not isolated, but are, instead, aspects of one and the same process.

During the 1960's, the various empires that existed—the French, Belgian, Portuguese, Dutch, and British—were all withdrawing direct control over dominions in Asia and Africa, and were either installing democratic republics in their place, or having them installed against their wishes by groups funded and organised by the USA, UK, or USSR. The British Empire's holdings were purposefully and swiftly converted to this new arrangement by British elites, with only a few territories proving to be a problem, such as South Africa and Rhodesia where the colonists resisted the changes to various degrees. British and American manoeuvring and support for opposition groups defeated these holdouts eventually. The other European empires also proved problematic, but UK and US pressure, under the guise of the International Community, defeated them as well. Notable examples include Portuguese holdings in West Africa and French holdings in Algeria. These newly democratic territories swiftly devolved into arenas of intense geopolitical conflict, and it is in this situation that we find the imperative to present the Western system of the International Community as preferable to the Soviet one in terms of racial equality. Within this environment of competition over equality and freedom, the CIA created the American Society of African Culture (AMSAC) in June 1954. This organisation was designed to promote American culture and anti-communism in the African territories.[9]

The integration of race issues with anti-communism was also evident in the actions of the elite in the United Kingdom. The initial central organisation for anti-racism in the UK, the Institute for Race Relations, was, in its beginnings, closely linked with the Ford Foundation, its biggest funder. It is claimed that the institution was inaugurated in the wake of a speech by Harry Hodson, and if we look at the speech we are not disappointed, as it accords with what we would expect from the Jouvenelian model. In the speech,[10] Hodson declares that "[t]here are two problems in world politics today which transcend all others. They are the struggle between Communism and liberal democracy, and the problem of race relations," with the danger being that communism may succeed in "enlisting most of the discontented or the non-European races on its side." Here, again, we have the direct link between the creation of cultural infrastructure and geopolitical conflict.

If, as predicted by the Jouvenelian model, this pattern of equalising culture is the result of a centralising Power, then we should be able to locate a similar centre of Power in our 20th century example. At this point, the reader may be confused since we don't seem to have a centre that fits this mould. Where, then, is the international centralising Power in our modern order? The answer is that while there is such a centre, it is not conscious. While many of these concepts have been developed in such a way that they presuppose a centre of Power at the international level, this centre has not been formally occupied, and instead merely exists in potentiality. The United Nations, and prior to this, the League of Nations, have not taken up this role, despite the desire of some that they do. Instead, it seems that a rather confused set of elites, operating across the Anglo-American world, have created this situation in a haphazard ideological way in the process of advancing their geopolitical interests. This odd combination of elites from both the USA and the UK began acting in unison during

---

9 For an account of the development of the American Society of African Culture (AMSAC), see Hugh Wilford, "Into Africa," in *The Mighty Wurlitzer: How the CIA Played America* (Cambridge: Harvard University Press, 2009), 197–224.

10 H.V. Hodson, "Race Relations in the Commonwealth," *International Affairs (Royal Institute of International Affairs 1944–)*, Vol. 26, No. 3 (July 1950): 305, https://www.jstor.org/stable/2607649.

the late 19th and early 20th centuries and not only worked towards, but actually succeeded in, aligning the geopolitical interests of both the British Empire and the USA, and in so doing, worked irrespective of formal institutions which they merely utilised as and when needed.

One of the more informative accounts of these elites during this period is provided by Inderjeet Parmar in *Think Tanks and Power in Foreign Policy* which applies Gramscian analysis to the roles played by two very important foreign policy institutions in the 20th century: the Council on Foreign Relations (CFR) in the USA, and the Royal Institute of International Affairs (RIIA) in the United Kingdom. According to Parmar, the institutions:

> ...played key roles in advance preparation and planning for the postwar world order. They were, and are, core components of their respective nations' foreign policy establishments and, some would claim, of an Anglo-American establishment. They are part of an elite network that connects corporate wealth, universities, philanthropic foundations, and official policymakers (Shoup and Minter, 1977; Schulzinger, 1984; Wala, 1994; Parmar, 1995b, 1999b, 2001).[11]

The origin of these institutions is informative. From the British angle, the narrative is provided in quite some detail by Carroll Quigley in *The Anglo-American Establishment*.[12] Here, a fortune bequeathed by the famous mining magnate, Cecil Rhodes, was turned into a pool of resources from which the specific goal of reintegrating the USA into the British Empire was pursued by Rhodes' protégé, Lord Alfred Milner, the founder of Milner's kindergarten.[13] The clique that was built with these resources was ably staffed by utopian Protestant Christians of the British elite who were amenable to this project. The most interesting of these was Milner's successor, Lionel Curtis, whose influence and power

---

11 Parmar, *Think Tanks*, 3.
12 Quigley, *The Anglo-American Establishment*.
13 Cecil Rhodes was a rabid proponent of the unification of what he saw as the Anglo-Saxon world and specifically desired the unification of the USA and the British Empire into a global empire as stated in his first will (1877) which stipulated the creation of a secret society devoted to "The extension of British rule throughout the world... [and]...the ultimate recovery of the United States of America as an integral part of a British Empire." ibid., 33.

through this network built by Milner was extensive.[14] He was successful at obtaining further funds from wealthy patrons, and continued to advance the overall goals of the group. It is this group of liberal imperialists that met and organised with the American delegation of Wilsonian internationalists, headed by Edward Mandell House, also known as Colonel House, at the Paris peace conference. Here, it was determined that close links on the issue of international affairs between the US and UK would be established; the primary result of these discussions being the creation of the CFR and the RIIA. Both institutions were funded with private donations or foundation funding, and both would go on to be incorporated into the governance of foreign affairs in their respective countries by the time of WWII.

From the US angle, the story is quite similar, and we see a number of actors forming around the fortunes bequeathed by US philanthropists, with elites from both sides of the Atlantic sharing:

> "Key, liberal 'core beliefs' congruent with their times: an uncritical attitude towards the character and virtues of scientific belief, and its applicability to social and international issues; liberal internationalism; a belief in the virtues of personal and institutional independence; public service; non-partisanship in foreign affairs; a belief in their own intellectual/social superiority, a deep seated elitism; shared religious backgrounds, however secularised, that schooled them in 'muscular Christianity'; an attitude of white, English-speaking people's racial superiority, expressed as 'Anglo-Saxonism'; and an unreflective attachment to the notions of 'manliness'"[15]

There are interesting first-hand accounts that point to the possibility that many actors in this environment on the British side were aware of what was occurring, and were happy to appeal to this utopian sensibility on the American side as a means to further the deepening of links, and to maintain international affairs

14 The list of 20th century developments attributable to, or influenced by, Curtis is formidable, and it is quite damning that his place in British history is almost completely ignored in standard histories.
15 Parmar, *Think Tanks*, 58–59.

to their joint benefit.[16] There is also record of British delegates
to the US purposefully reframing the collaboration between the
British Empire and the USA in internationalist language, such
as the following from a British delegate to an Institute of Pacific
Relations conference in 1942 who noted that:

> ...in the terms of the United Nations if it is to make an ap-
> peal. In the event, Britain and the United States may share
> the major burden, but it must be in a world organisation,
> *using an international vocabulary.*[17]

This internationalist movement was already in transition before this point, with the casting of this alliance in Anglo-Saxon
racial terms, as seen in the earlier aims of Cecil Rhodes, being
whittled away and transformed into cultural claims, something
we also see with political science in this period.[18] Geopolitical

16   Parmar, *Think Tanks*, 72–74.

17   ibid., 94.

18   There was a fairly widespread belief among political scientists in the late 19th
century and the early 20th century that American and British political institutions
had their roots in Teutonic history. This "Teutonic Principle," predictably from a
Jouvenelian angle, does not seem to have been eclipsed by alternative schools of
thought due to successful debate or any kind of intellectual victory, but instead
seems to have fallen afoul of geopolitical conflict, specifically in WWI. It was the
entry of the USA into this war against Germany which turned authorities against
this school of thought for obviously practical reasons. Consider James Farr's following assessment of the fate of the Teutonic Principle:
"The war breached the affinity and affection that many American scholars felt for
German ideas and ideals that resonated with their own science of the state. It certainly ended the American embrace of the Teutonic principle in almost all forms;
positive references to Teutonism or things Teutonic fell from use nearly for good.
Tellingly, though, Burgess was an exception, as was Schaper. Their sympathies for
the German cause cost the latter his job at Minnesota and earned the former the
charge of being "an American perverted by too close contact with Germany and
German ideas," not to mention a "doddering old idiot." In 1917, Dunning assailed
"the Anglo-Saxon militant, the Teuton rampant, and the Aryan eternally trium-
phant." For their war work, Willoughby battled Prussian political philosophy and
Garner judged guilty the German war code. In creating the Committee on Public Information (CPI), the Wilson administration offered employment to writers
of pamphlets like "Lieber and Schurz: Two Loyal Americans of German Birth."
More significantly, the CPI brought historians and political scientists into direct service of the American state as propagandists, including Garner, Lippmann,
Munroe Smith, and Merriam (as CPI field head in Rome). Hart served in similar
capacity for the National Security League. Thus did the historical scientists of
politics in America go to war; and thus did propaganda come to occupy a central

power requirements were observably determinative of intellectual culture, and drove the need to transform this language from one of Anglo-Saxon syncretism to one of universalist international syncretism. As Parmar notes, this was so as to accomplish a "far broader consumption (particularly in the ethnically diverse USA and to bolster the anti-Axis nations)[*sic*] into some form of Anglo-American amity."[19]

These elites, devout Protestants, adhered to a belief in the rule of law and democracy, but these beliefs, as we have seen in earlier chapters, are centralising beliefs by default, which demand a centralised Power structure.[20] As a result, these elites formed a centralising pattern of authority, even if not consciously and purposefully. This pattern of behaviour continues down to our present world order where our current progressive elite seem to have a sincere and devout belief in the moral significance of such things as human rights and democracy, yet do not understand, or do not acknowledge, that such universalised concepts demand, by default, a governance structure which incorporates the entirety of mankind.

The result of this complex—and, at times, perplexing—in-

---

place in their conceptions of civic education and public opinion. Their erstwhile identities having been challenged and changed, political scientists emerged from the Great War ready to rethink, without abandoning, history, the state, and the principles of their science."
James Farr, "The Historical Science(s) of Politics: The Principles, Association, and Fate of an American Discipline," in *Modern Political Science: Anglo-American Exchanges since 1880*, eds. Robert Adcock, Mark Bevir and Shannon C. Stimson (Princeton: Princeton University Press, 2009), 96.

19 Parmar, *Think Tanks*, 71.

20 On this point, it is interesting to consider Carroll Quigley's claims that the Milner Group saw themselves as, in some sense, inheritors of the values of Athenian liberty, as Quigley writes: "History for this Group, and especially for Curtis, presented itself as an age-long struggle between the principles of autocracy and the principles of commonwealth, between the forces of darkness and the forces of light, between Asiatic theocracy and European freedom." Quigley, *The Anglo-American Establishment,* 133. Compare this to Jouvenel's recognition that the Athenians were more centralised than any Asiatic theocracy in a note for chapter VIII in *On Power*: "It is no use bringing up against me the cliché about the despotic power of Xerxes going down before the liberty of the Athenians. When I refer here to a larger, more total Power, I mean a Power which demands and obtains relatively more from its people. It is certain that in this respect the Power in the Greek cities over the citizens was far in excess of that of the Great King over his subjects." Jouvenel, *On Power*, 397.

terplay of internal political conflict, sincere belief in anarchistic systems, and geopolitical necessity is the current world order, in which, for all intents and purposes, those within the Western world are directed towards an international Power centre which does not formally exist. Each individual is considered, in the modern liberal scheme, to be in possession of universalised characteristics which imply this world Power, but which are, in reality, guaranteed in a collective manner by nation-state level institutions. It is within this maelstrom that we find human rights, LGBT rights, Islamism, immigration, and every other facet of modernity linked to progressivism, walking hand in hand with corporate, military, and bureaucratic expansion in a rather mindless growth.

The picture I have thus far painted of our modern order is far from flattering to our current elite, an elite who appear to be rather ignorant of the nature of their role in modern governance. It is also likely to prove rather controversial in that it implies that many of the beliefs of this modern elite are fundamentally based on reflexive political conflict, and lack any underlying rational basis. As distressing a conclusion as this may be, it is one faithful to the Jouvenelian model.

Despite the very obvious intellectual bankruptcy of the liberal order, this order is, despite constant pronouncements to the contrary, dominant, and increasingly so, especially in the Western world. It is not clear what institutions and patrons exist who are in a position to offer a serious alternative, and while there are numerous supposedly illiberal reactions in places such as Hungary, Israel, and now the USA with the presidency of Donald Trump, these movements are remarkably shallow from a Jouvenelian angle. These orders do not offer any major systemic alternative to liberal systems, nor is it clear that they are in a position to do so. It follows from the obvious Jouvenelian connection of the geopolitical environment with internal cultural developments that any system of political thought which hopes to address the obvious problems of the modern order must be international in scope, and thus far, nothing of this kind has been advanced. Such a system must at once address the issues of internal governance which grant the proponents of liberalism so much power, and must also offer a vision of a geopolitical order which mediates the relationships of the various orders that exist in such a way as to ensure that these orders encourage and foster the goals being pursued, and do not begin to reproduce the systemic basis of liberalism due to geopolitical conflict.

POSTFACE

As this work has been primarily concerned with making the case that the Jouvenelian model surpasses modern political models, there has been an unavoidably negative and critical pattern to the arguments made. This criticism, directed at the modern forms of thought and categories of existence which underpin modern political thought, has been necessary, as it is only by a process of demonstrating the superior functionality of one model as against the alternatives that a robust case can be made for the wholesale rejection of these alternative models. Within this work, the points of comparison chosen to support this attempt were the provision of Jouvenelian explanations of political phenomena, and the ability to account for the historical contingency of ideas. Such a state of affairs is comparable to the process by which scientific models succeed other models, wherein success is gauged by the greater explanatory power inherent in the newer models or by the failure of older models to explain certain phenomena at all. Of primary importance in this process has been the attempt to account for the development of concepts such as the individual and sovereignty—developments for which adherents of modernity were themselves unable to account except in vague or frankly mystical terms—and to provide an account of how cultural trends and revolutions occur.

Given this focus on critiquing modernity and its fundamental concepts, the task of exploring the implications of the acceptance of Jouvenelian theory for the current liberal order, or what form an order cognisant of the Jouvenelian dynamic might take in a post-liberal world, has not been attempted. I shall attempt to briefly and partially remedy this here, but am under no illusions that I will be able to provide an exhaustive account.

If we begin with the implications of this theory for our current order, we are immediately faced with the obvious fact that the Jouvenelian model predicts that, under normal circumstances, Jouvenelian thought will itself likely be systematically and comprehensively incapable of reaching any sort of institutional significance. We exist within an order which not only has no need for Jouvenel's insights, but has been predicated on actively obfuscating the mechanisms of centralisation made clear by the Jouvenelian model. The modern liberal order, an order revealed by Jouvenel as a hyper-centralised one that has been patronising cultural trends and political theories in adherence to this hyper-centralisation, has no incentive to offer patronage and institutional existence to a body of thought which exposes this process of power. It is a fallacious belief in the natural, anarchistic flowering of culture independent of logistical infrastructure, a belief propagated by this very same system, which allows this process to occur without the recognition of the system's inhabitants that they are determining culture by their infrastructural support of specific bodies of thought. In such an environment, the lack of widespread acknowledgment of Jouvenelian theory can quite comfortably be ascribed to a lack of relevance or accuracy. Meanwhile, massive and sustained funding of identity politics, gender theory, liberal political science, and other systems of thought favoured by foundations and academia will continue apace as though it is entirely neutral, or simply lending assistance to level the playing field for otherwise impoverished actors.

On a more positive note, it may be that we are living in a period within which technological change and its destabilising effects are making it possible to circumvent this funding and institutional infrastructure of the modern liberal order. We now live in world in which it is possible to freely obtain the intellectual resources previously available only to those within academia. As such, a school of thought can, with some effort, be developed and maintained online despite its members living vast distances apart, thereby negating the necessity of centralised academic departments and the funding implicit to them. Further to this, the ability to independently publish works and to communicate to a worldwide audience is now greater than ever, and works such as the present one can be created and distributed to this potential audience without the need for foundation grants or access to the standard media channels that underpin our current order. In short, the internet allows, for the time being, the creation of a virtual infrastructure which can compete with that which forms the skeleton of the liberal order. We can see this in how such platforms as Twitter or YouTube can allow a single individual to reach audiences that were previously the preserve of select media. How long this state of affairs will last is an important question, and, so far, this window of opportunity has been squandered with rather unimportant and frivolous illiberal political thought. Despite the relative impotence of this illiberalism, it has served to encourage the development of new means of infrastructural control, such as simply denying certain actors online hosting or even access to payment processing systems. This is a clear demonstration of the significance of finance, infrastructure, and ultimately power, to culture—a point which is becoming more and more obvious with each passing day.

Assuming that this possibility of forming virtual infrastructure continues, and that, as a result, a level of acceptance can be gained among intellectuals independent of the standard avenues of culture such as foundation grants, academic institutions, and traditional media, the subsequent problem predicted by the Jouvenelian model is that this body of Jouvenelian thought will come to be seen as subversive to liberal centralising power, and will, therefore, be seen as a threat by the elite, and rejected on spurious grounds. In such a situation, it is quite likely that the arguments in this work would find fertile grounds among centres of power which are generally opposed to centralising Power, and would provide intellectual support for the revolt of the middle that is currently occurring. In chapter 11, we noted that there are various anti-globalist movements throughout the world which are attempting to deal with the problem of uncontrolled centralisation, whether they recognise it in Jouvenelian terms or not, by attempt-

POSTFACE

ing to assert the independence of nation-states against a globalis-
ing and centralising international bureaucratic and capitalist elite;
however, what the Jouvenelian theory tells us is that these attempts, in failing to appreciate the Jouvenelian nature of political
structures, are making self-defeating mistakes which merely work
to entrench the very problems they are seeking to remedy. These
movements fail to develop sophisticated political theory to act as
a blueprint for sustained and wide-ranging institutional changes,
and clearly internalise naive beliefs about the nature of power—
beliefs which flow from modern understandings of the nature of
power propagated by the very system of power they are seeking
to alter. Upon obtaining positions of influence and control, these
actors become embroiled in Jouvenelian structural conflict which
they do not understand and have no idea how to reform, and they
do not then move to secure the structure of power in such a way
as to mitigate Jouvenelian conflict.

This all obviously presumes that any Jouvenelian-premised
school of thought becomes embodied in centres of power oppos-
ing the centralisation of power, but such an assumption is not
entirely warranted, as it may be the case that those in the liberal
structure see the need to stabilise the current order in response to
this threat from nationalist movements and the destabilisation of
current technologies. Such a development would represent something along the lines of an internal transition to a formalisation of
the current institutions, but such an event, while possible, is, currently, highly unlikely. The reason it is so unlikely is that to maintain any sort of power within the current order requires that those
in these positions either hold, or at the very least sincerely pretend
to hold, liberal beliefs which have reached a rather extreme point.
For example, for anyone currently in a position of power to even
entertain a serious debate as to the Jouvenelian nature of the civil
rights era, to entertain the closure of tax-exempt foundations, or
to seriously question the nature of current economic structures, is
far beyond the realm of the possible in the current political environment. It would seem that the current political structures of the
liberal order are far too fractured, far too riddled with conflict, and
far too sclerotic to be subject to internal redirection at the level
required for adoption of Jouvenelian theory. Yet, it is only by appeal to some section of this governmental system and the patrons

within it that any sort of serious change can occur, and it would seem that in this situation the only hope for such change rests in supporting a hyper-centralised government capable of making wide, sweeping alterations to this order. In America, for example, this could come in the form of a strengthened presidency, with its own structures of government capable of acting unilaterally, but as we have seen with the progressive era, such a thing led to many of the current norms. Granted, Jouvenel himself cautioned against thought which sought to provide justification for utilisation of a centralised power centre to reshape orders, but given current technological and organisational patterns and the total and utter failure of attempts to counter this centralisation, might it not prove unavoidably necessary? We could go even further and point out that it has been attempts to formulate intellectual rejections of centralisation, such as Rousseau's "will of the people," or Lockean consent, which have formed the most effective and confusing disguises whereby this power has expanded exponentially, and often entirely irrationally. Paradoxically, it would seem that a clear recognition and acceptance of this centrality could prove to be the more effective means by which this centralisation can be negotiated. The act of formalising the relationships currently in existence would logically lead to a reduction in the need for centralised power centres to engage in the Jouvenelian mechanism to shape a given order. With a clear recognition of the validity of this central power altering orders as necessary, the warping effect of power in all areas of existence would be better accounted for, and a more coherent and possibly non-coercive order could be instituted.

This alternative route of actively favouring the centralisation process, or of merely accepting it as inevitable, offers a potential escape from the paradox of Jouvenelian thought lacking appeal to patrons in the power structure. It is also, arguably, the more reasonable and coherent theoretical position to take, given the Jouvenelian model. We find ourselves within a drastically centralised order, and it is only from the recognition of this, rather than a hopeful belief that this is not the case, that a start can be made in mastering the situation and moving to one which is more desirable. By capturing and controlling this centralised point of power, and by creating an environment such that its inhabitants can be discouraged from engaging in Jouvenelian conflict and the attendant ethical and intellectual confusion which follows in its wake, we can hopefully allow for the return of something approaching rationality in the practice of governance.

All of this is obviously highly speculative, and it is difficult to predict just which patrons may find use for this theory, and in what circumstances. As we have seen in earlier chapters, it has been as a result of conflict and geopolitical peculiarities that some of the more unlikely cultural developments have occurred, and it is impossible to predict what kinds of conflicts may occur in the future that may be of benefit to those attempting to bring about a Jouvenel-informed order. New resources may be discovered, or old resources may come into greater demand due to technological developments; strategic errors or natural disasters can also play their part in unforeseen lines of conflict. What can, however, be said with certainty from the Jouvenelian angle is that patrons will, indeed, be needed, and that no political change can be predicated on organic revolt from the ground up. Revolutions and popular movements emphatically do not rise to success without patronage, and anyone under illusions on this point would do well to compare the singular success of the Arab Spring protestors to the complete and utter failure of the French "yellow vest" movement. The yellow vest protests have lasted significantly longer than the Arab Spring protests and covered a far greater area, and yet their impact has been inconsequential for the simple reason that one set of protests had patrons and the other did not, which brings us to the question of becoming worthy of patronage.

Assuming that a Jouvenelian-informed order should come into being, how, then, would reforms derived from Jouvenelian theory appear? Internally, such reforms would have to reconfigure the relationship of centres of power within a given order through a comprehensive rejection of categories of existence intrinsic to the modern liberal state, and of the unconstrained Jouvenelian conflict inherent in its order. Such concepts as the public/private distinction, the economy, civil society, and all other systems which entrench fallacious beliefs regarding the nature of authority would, naturally, be significantly reinterpreted.

To achieve such wide-ranging reform would require alternative institutions willing and able to act at the behest of those in power seeking to make such changes. The modern order brought into being by progressive actors in the early 20th century achieved as much through the use of institutions in the private sphere, utilising foundations funded by private money to act as active arms of governance where the current system proved obstructive, and it may be the case that such a stratagem would, again, be required, which presents something of a conundrum, given that these avenues of funding not only are, by their nature, culturally liberal, but exacerbate the Jouvenelian centralisation process, and would thereby serve to undermine their own privileged positions. This is not to say that any Jouvenelian order would be hostile to markets and corporations, but, rather, that this order would be highly critical of current claims which grant these economic entities and the wealth they hold special privileges that allow their owners to act in extremely damaging ways. It may be that some of these privileged individuals would recognise the ultimate benefit in financially supporting such an endeavour, or it may be that alternative forms of financing are required, whatever they prove to be. In either case, it seems inevitable that to obtain power, and to institute reforms, would require a cynical utilisation of current categories in the process of moving towards their abolishment.

It follows from this analysis that the immediate concern for any attempt to further Jouvenelian modes of thought would be to create entities worthy of patronage should the opportunity arise. Whilst such structures would, undoubtedly, be limited due to a lack of major patronage, the very fact that they exist in any sort of form would place them within the possible notice of patrons who could offer the promise of greater embodiment as serious institutions. Such entities should not be subversive and opposed to current authorities, but rather amenable to those in power under necessary circumstances. Possible examples would include the creation of media entities such as publishing houses and news channels, journals, think tanks, educational institutions, and governmental structures in waiting, all linked by a shared basis in Jouvenelian doctrine, and which offer serious and sophisticated theoretical responses to problems that current political theory is simply unable even to comprehend, let alone respond to.

Another pertinent point that requires attention, beyond simply the internal structures and relations which a given central power would need to reform, is the international order within which the power exists. It follows from the Jouvenelian model that for any internal changes to be maintained, international norms of behaviour would need to be reformulated in order to remove the impetus for the current forms of governance. These norms would have to be such that conflict is minimised and formalisation of power in neighbouring orders is encouraged to the fullest so as to reduce the potential of various powers engaging in the Jouvenelian dynamic. Such an international order would stand in stark contrast to the internal order led by the International Community which actively discourages the formalisation of governance and the responsibility which would attend this formalisation. This is something which the international order perversely does on the basis of democracy and liberal capitalism, systems which are claimed to provide accountability through elections, profit motives, and choice, but which, in reality, shield those in positions of power from accountability. In the realm of electoral politics this is achieved by aggressive control of media narratives and population replacement through mass immigration, and in the realm of the economy this is achieved by the illusion of contractual parity between unequal actors, the illusion of equality in the marketplace, and in the subsidisation of losses incurred by major actors with political connections. That this is the case is clear for all to see from events ranging from the encouragement of mass immigration in support of progressive parties to the bailout of banks following the financial crisis of 2008.

Jouvenelian thought, and any possible Jouvenelian order, would, therefore, have to be international in scope, and cannot merely be resigned to localised existence within an international order in which the Jouvenelian dynamic of hyper-centralisation is dominant. All incentives for uncontrolled and irrational centralisation both internal and external would need to be carefully mitigated. There would, therefore, have to be an international cross-network of actors offering mutual assistance to those in other orders so as to encourage the collective security of all against the predation of actors engaging, knowingly or not, in Jouvenelian destabilisation.

BIBLIOGRAPHY

Alexander, Christopher. *Tunisia: From Stability to Revolution in the Maghreb*. New York: Routledge, 2016.

Al-Rasheed, Madawi. *A History of Saudi Arabia*. New York: Cambridge University Press, 2010.

Anderson, Gary M., and Robert D. Tollison Bd. "Ideology, Interest Groups, and the Repeal of the Corn Laws." *Zeitschrift für die gesamte Staatswissenschaft / Journal of Institutional and Theoretical Economics*, 141, H.2. (June 1985): 197–212. https://www.jstor.org/stable/40750831.

Apodaca, Clair. *Understanding U.S. Human Rights Policy: A Paradoxical Legacy*. New York: Taylor & Francis, 2013.

Aristotle. *Aristotle's Ethics for English Readers*. Translated by H. Rackham. New York: Barnes & Noble, 1952.

———. *Politics*. Translated by H. Rackham. Cambridge: Harvard University Press, 1959.

Associated Press in Washington. "US secretly created 'Cuban Twitter' to stir unrest and undermine government." *The Guardian*, April 3, 2014. https://www.theguardian.com/world/2014/apr/03/us-cuban-twitter-zunzuneo-stir-unrest.

Avi-Yonah, Reuven S. "The Cyclical Transformations of the Corporate Form: A Historical Perspective on Corporate Social Responsibility." *Del-*

aware *Journal of Corporate Law*, Vol. 30, No. 3 (2005): 767–818. https://dx.doi.org/10.2139/ssrn.672601.

Bach, Volker. "Markets for Mercenaries: Supplying Armies in Sixteenth-Century Germany." In *Food & Markets: Proceedings of the Oxford Symposium on Food and Cookery 2014,* edited by Mark Williams, 35–43, London: Prospect Books, 2015.

Berman, Harold J. *Law and Revolution: The Formation of the Western Legal Tradition*. Cambridge: Harvard University Press, 1983.

Berndtson, Erkki. "Behavioralism: Origins of the Concept." Presentation, 17th International Political Science Association World Congress, Seoul, Korea, August 17–21, 1997.

Bevir, Mark, Shannon C. Stimson and Robert Adcock. *Modern Political Science: Anglo-American Exchanges Since 1880*. Princeton: Princeton University Press, 2007.

Blakely, Jason William. "Three Political Philosophers Debate Social Science: Leo Strauss, Alasdair MacIntyre, and Charles Taylor." PhD diss., University of California, Berkeley, 2013.

Bonfiglioli, Chiara. "The First UN World Conference on Women (1975) as a Cold War Encounter: Recovering Anti-Imperialist, Non-Aligned and Socialist Genealogies." *Filozofija i drustvo,* 27(3) (January 2016): 521–41. https://doi.org/10.2298/FID1603521B.

Bowen, Wayne H. *The History of Saudi Arabia*. Santa Barbara: Greenwood Press, 2008.

Brinkley, Douglas. "The Man Who Kept King's Secrets." *Vanityfair.com,* April, 2006, http://www.vanityfair.com/news/politics/2014/01/clarence-jones-martin-luther-king-jr-secrets.

Butler, Henry N. "The Contractual Theory of the Corporation." *George Mason University Law Review*, Col. 11, No. 4, (Summer 1989): 99–123.

Carlyle, R.W. and A.J. Carlyle. *A History of Mediaeval Political Theory in the West, Vol VI: Political Theory from 1300 to 1600*. London: Blackwood, 1936.

Cavanaugh, William T. "A Fire Strong Enough to Consume the House: The Wars of Religion and the Rise of the State." *Modern Theology* 11, Issue 4, (October 1995): 397–420. https://doi.org/10.1111/j.1468-0025.1995.tb00073.x.

———. The Myth of Religious Violence: Secular Ideology and the Roots of Modern Conflict. Oxford: Oxford University Press, 2009.

Central Intelligence Agency. *Studies in Intelligence: Origins of the Congress for Cultural Freedom, 1949–50.* Declassified draft study. Date unknown. https://web.archive.org/web/20060616213245/http://cia.gov/csi/studies/95unclass/Warner.html.

Ciepley, David. "Beyond Public and Private: Toward a Political Theory of the Corporation." *American Political Science Review*, Vol. 107, No. 1 (February 2013): 139–58.

———. "The Corporate Contradictions of Neoliberalism." *American Affairs*, Vol. 1, No. 2, (Summer 2017), https://americanaffairsjournal.org/2017/05/corporate-contradictions-neoliberalism/.

Coase, R.H. "The Nature of the Firm." *Economica*, New Series, Vol. 4, Issue 16 (November 1937): 386–405. https://doi.org/10.1111/j.1468-0335.1937.tb00002.x.

Cobain, Ian. "'Mind control': The secret UK government blueprints shaping post-terror planning." *Middle East Eye*, May 22, 2019. https://www.middleeasteye.net/news/mind-control-secret-british-government-blueprints-shaping-post-terror-planning.

Coll, Steve. Ghost Wars: The Secret History of the CIA, Afghanistan, and bin Laden, from the Soviet Invasion to September 10, 2001. London: Penguin Books, 2005.

Coulanges, Numa Denis Fustel de. *The Ancient City: A Study on the Religion, Laws, and Institutions of Greece and Rome.* Perth: Imperium Press, 2019.

Curtis, Mark. *Secret Affairs: Britain's Collusion with Radical Islam.* London: Serpent's Tail, 2018.

Cuttica, Cesare. "Sir Robert Filmer (1588–1653) and the Condescension of Posterity: Historiographical Interpretations." *Intellectual History Review*, Vol. 21, Issue 2 (2011): 195–208. https://doi.org/10.1080/17496977.2011.574345.

Daley, J.L. *The Political Theory of John Wyclif.* Chicago: Loyola Press, 1962.

Daniels, Alex. "Ford Shifts Grant Making to Focus Entirely on Inequality." *The Chronicle of Philanthropy*, June, 11, 2015. https://www.philanthropy.com/article/Ford-Shifts-Grant-Making-to/230839/.

Darwin, Charles. *The Origin of Species*. New York: Simon & Schuster Paperbacks, 2009.

Embassy Egypt. "APRIL 6 ACTIVIST DESCRIBES GOE HA-RASSMENT, REQUESTS INFORMATION ON YOUTH MOVE-MENTS SUMMIT," Wikileaks Cable: 08CAIRO2431_a, dated November 26, 2008, https://wikileaks.org/plusd/cables/08CAIRO2431_a. html.

———. "APRIL 6 ACTIVIST ON HIS U.S. VISIT AND REGIME CHANGE IN EGYPT," Wikileaks Cable: 08CAIRO2572_a, dated December 30, 2008, https://wikileaks.org/plusd/cables/08CAIRO2572_a. html.

Embassy Morocco. "SECRETARY CHALLENGES BMENA CIVIL SOCIETY," Wikileaks Cable: 09RABAT921_a, dated November 22, 2009, https://wikileaks.org/plusd/cables/09RABAT921_a.html.

Embassy Tunisia. "DAS CARPENTER'S ROUNDTABLE WITH TU-NISIAN CIVIL SOCIETY," Wikileaks Cable: 07TUNIS102_a, dated January 23, 2007, https://wikileaks.org/plusd/cables/07TUNIS102_a. html.

———. "TROUBLED TUNISIA: WHAT SHOULD WE DO?," Wikileaks Cable: 09TUNIS492_a, dated July 17, 2009, https://search. wikileaks.org/plusd/cables/09TUNIS492_a.html.

———. "UNION LEADER HIGHLIGHTS SHARED VAL-UES, DISILLUSION WITH US POLICY," Wikileaks Cable: 07TUNIS246_a, dated February 22, 2007, https://wikileaks.org/plusd/ cables/07TUNIS246_a.html.

Farr, James. "The History of Political Science." *American Journal of Political Science*, Vol. 32, No. 4 (November, 1988): 1175–95. https://www.jstor. org/stable/i310473.

———. "The Historical Science(s) of Politics: The Principles, Association, and Fate of an American Discipline." In *Modern Political Science: Anglo-American Exchanges since 1880*, edited by Robert Adcock, Mark Bevir and Shannon C. Stimson, 66–96. Princeton: Princeton University Press, 2009.

Figgis, John Neville. *The Divine Right of Kings*. Cambridge: University Press, 1914.

Friedman, Milton, and Rose D. Friedman. *Capitalism and Freedom*. Chicago: University of Chicago Press, 2002.

Foucault, Michel. *Discipline and Punish: The Birth of the Prison.* Translated by Alan Sheridan. New York: Vintage Books, 1995.

Gaither Jr., H.R. *Report of the Study for the Ford Foundation Policy and Program.* Detroit, Michigan: Ford Foundation, 1949.

Gans, Eric. *The Origin of Language: A New Edition.* New York: Spuyten Duyvil Publishing, 2019.

Ganser, Daniele. *NATO's Secret Armies: Operation GLADIO and Terrorism in Western Europe.* London: Frank Cass, 2005.

Graeber, David. *Debt: The First 5,000 Years.* New York: Melville House, 2011.

Graeber, David, and Marshall Sahlins. *On Kings.* Chicago: Hau Books, 2017.

Grimm, Dieter. *Sovereignty: The Origin and Future of a Political and Legal Concept.* New York: Columbia University Press, 2015.

Girard, René. *Deceit, Desire, and the Novel: Self and Other in Literary Structure.* Baltimore: Johns Hopkins University Press, 2010.

Grosse, Peter. *Continuing the Inquiry: The Council on Foreign Relations From 1921 to 1996.* New York: Council on Foreign Relations Press, 1996.

Guilhot, Nicolas. *The Invention of International Relations Theory: Realism, the Rockefeller Foundation, and the 1954 Conference on Theory.* New York: Columbia University Press, 2011.

Henderson, Ernest F. *Select Historical Documents of the Middle Ages.* London: George Bell and Sons, 1910.

Higgins, Andrew. "How Israel Helped to Spawn Hamas." *The Wall Street Journal,* January 24, 2009, https://www.wsj.com/articles/SB123275572295011847.

Hobbes, Thomas. *De Cive: The English Version.* Oxford: Clarendon Press, 1983.

Hodson, H.V. "Race Relations in the Commonwealth." *International Affairs (Royal Institute of International Affairs 1944–),* Vol. 26, No. 3 (July 1950): 305–315. https://www.jstor.org/stable/2607649.

BIBLIOGRAPHY

Holt, Mack P. *The French Wars of Religion, 1562–1629*. Cambridge: Cambridge University Press, 2007.

Horwitz, Morton J. "The History of the Public/Private Distinction." *University of Pennsylvania Law Review*, Vol. 130 (1982): 1423–28. https://www.jstor.org/stable/3311976.

Hudson, Richard. "The Judicial Reforms of the Reign of Henry II." *Michigan Law Review*, Vol. 9, No. 5 (March 1911): 385–95. http://www.jstor.org/stable/1275164.

Huxley, T.H. Review of *The Origin of Species*, by Charles Darwin. *Westminster Review*, Vol. 17, (January 1860): 541–70.

———. "The Struggle for Existence: A Programme." *Popular Science Monthly*, Vol. 32 (April 1888): 732–50.

Jilani, Zaid. "In Secret Goldman Sachs Speech, Hillary Clinton Admitted No-Fly Zone Would 'Kill a Lot of Syrians.'" *The Intercept*, October 10, 2016. https://theintercept.com/2016/10/10/in-secret-goldman-sachs-speech-hillary-clinton-admitted-no-fly-zone-would-kill-a-lot-of-syrians/.

Jouvenel, Bertrand de. *On Power: Its Nature and the History of Its Growth*. Boston: Beacon Press, 1962.

Judicial Watch, *Department of Defense Information Report*, 14-L-0552/DIA/ 289, accessed March 3, 2017. http://www.judicialwatch.org/wp-content/uploads/2015/05/Pg.-291-Pgs.-287-293-JW-v-DOD-and-State-14-812-DOD-Release-2015-04-10-final-version11.pdf.

King, Martin Luther. Martin Luther King to Nelson A. Rockefeller, November 1, 1965. The King Center Archive. Accessed March 28, 2017. http://thekingcenter.org/archive/document/letter-mlk-nelson-rockefeller.

Kirkpatrick, David D., and David E. Sanger. "A Tunisian-Egyptian Link That Shook Arab History." *The New York Times*, February 13, 2011. http://www.nytimes.com/2011/02/14/world/middleeast/14egypt-tunisia-protests.html?pagewanted=all&_r=0.

Korey, William. *Taking on the World's Repressive Regimes: The Ford Foundation's International Human Rights Policies and Practices*. New York: Palgrave Macmillan, 2007.

Lavelle, Brian M. *Fame, Money, and Power: The Rise of Peisistratos and*

"Democratic" Tyranny at Athens. Ann Arbor: University of Michigan Press, 2005.

Lepenies, Philipp. *The Power of a Single Number: A Political History of GDP*. New York: Columbia University Press, 2016.

Locke, John. *Two Treatises of Government and A Letter Concerning Toleration*. New Haven: Yale University Press, 2003.

Luther, Martin "An Open Letter To The Christian Nobility Concerning the Reform of the Christian Estate (1520)," In *Works of Martin Luther: With Introductions and Notes, Volume II*. Philadelphia: A.J. Holman Company, 1915.

Lyttkens, Carl Hampus. *Economic Analysis of Institutional Change in Ancient Greece, Politics, Taxation and Rational Behaviour*. London: Routledge, 2015.

MacAskill, Ewan. "US confirms it asked Twitter to stay open to help Iran protesters." *The Guardian*, June 17, 2009. https://www.theguardian.com/world/2009/jun/17/obama-iran-twitter.

MacIntyre, Alasdair C. *A Short History of Ethics: A History of Moral Philosophy from the Homeric Age to the Twentieth Century*. New York: Simon & Schuster, 1996.

———. *After Virtue: A Study in Moral Theory*. Notre Dame: University of Notre Dame Press, 2007.

———. *First Principles, Final Ends, and Contemporary Philosophical Issues*. Milwaukee: Marquette University, 1990.

———. *Whose Justice? Which Rationality?* Notre Dame: University of Notre Dame Press, 1988.

McGrade, Arthur Stephen. *The Political Thought of William of Ockham: Personal and Institutional Principles*. Cambridge: Cambridge University Press, 2002.

McCready, William D. "Papal *Plenitudo Potestatis* and the Source of Temporal Authority in Late Medieval Papal Hierocratic Theory." *Speculum*, Vol. 48, No. 4, (October 1973): 654–74.

McNally, David. *Political Economy and the Rise of Capitalism: A Reinterpretation*. Berkeley: University of California Press, 1988.

McVeigh, Tracy. "'Recruiter' of UK jihadis: I regret opening the way to Isis." *The Guardian*, June 13, 2015. https://www.theguardian.com/world/2015/jun/13/godfather-of-british-jihadists-admits-we-opened-to-way-to-join-isis.

Michels, Robert. *Political Parties: A Sociological Study of the Oligarchical Tendencies of Modern Democracy.* Batoche Books: Ontario, 2001.

Milne, J.G. "The Economic Policy of Solon." *Hesperia: The Journal of the American School of Classical Studies at Athens*, Vol. 14, No. 3 (July-September, 1945): 230–45. https://www.jstor.org/stable/146709.

Mitchell, Thomas N. *Democracy's Beginning: The Athenian Story.* New Haven: Yale University Press, 2015.

Morris, Colin. *The Papal Monarchy: The Western Church from 1050 to 1250.* Oxford: Clarendon Press, 1989.

Nardi, Paolo. "Relations with Authority." In *A History of the University in Europe*, edited by Walter Rüegg, 77–106. Cambridge: Cambridge University Press, 1992.

Neier, Aryeh. "Brown v. Board of Ed: Key Cold War Weapon." *Reuters*, May 14, 2014. http://blogs.reuters.com/great-debate/2014/05/14/brown-v-board-of-ed-key-cold-war-weapon/.

———. *The International Human Rights Movement: A History.* Princeton: Princeton University Press, 2012.

Nixon, Ron. "U.S. Groups Helped Nurture Arab Uprisings." *The New York Times*, April 14, 2011. http://www.nytimes.com/2011/04/15/world/15aid.html?_r=3&pagewanted=1&emc=eta1.

Odlozilnik, O. "Wycliffe's Influence on Eastern and Central Europe." *Slavonic Review*, VII (1929): 634–48.

Ostwald, Martin. *From Popular Sovereignty to the Sovereignty of Law: Law, Society, and Politics in Fifth Century Athens.* Berkeley: University of California Press, 1986.

Paine, Thomas. *Common Sense.* Philadelphia: Robert Bell, 1776.

Parmar, Inderjeet. *Think Tanks and Power in Foreign Policy: A Comparative Study of the Role and Influence of the Council on Foreign Relations and the Royal Institute of International Affairs, 1939–1945.* Basingstoke: Palgrave Macmillan, 2004.

Patterson, James T. *Brown v. Board of Education: A Civil Rights Milestone and Its Troubled Legacy.* New York: Oxford University Press, 2001.

Pedrick, Clare. "CIA ORGANIZED SECRET ARMY IN WESTERN EUROPE." *The Washington Post*, November 14, 1990. https://www.washingtonpost.com/archive/politics/1990/11/14/cia-organized-secret-army-in-western-europe/e0305101-97b9-4494-bc18-d89f42497d85/?utm_term=.a2c2f1b2ff63.

Pennington, K. "Law, Legislative Authority, and Theories of Government, 1150–1300." In *The Cambridge History of Medieval Political Thought, c.350–c.1450*, edited by J.H. Burns, 424–53. Cambridge: University Press, 1988.

Pickering, Mary. *Auguste Comte: An Intellectual Biography, Volume One.* Cambridge: Cambridge University Press, 1993.

———. *Auguste Comte: An Intellectual Biography, Volume Two.* Cambridge: Cambridge University Press, 2009.

———. *Auguste Comte: An Intellectual Biography, Volume Three.* Cambridge: Cambridge University Press, 2009.

Pocock, J.G.A. *The Ancient Constitution and the Feudal Law: A Study of English Thought in the Seventeenth Century.* Cambridge: Cambridge University Press, 1987.

Podesta, John. "Re: opening for a Catholic Spring? just musing…" Email message to Sandy Newman and Tara McGuinness, February 11, 2012. https://wikileaks.org/podesta-emails/emailid/57579.

Pomeroy, Sarah B. *Goddesses, Whores, Wives and Slaves: Women in Classical Antiquity.* London: Hale, 1975.

Pospieszna, Paulina. *Democracy Assistance from the Third Wave: Polish Engagement in Belarus and Ukraine.* Pittsburgh: University of Pittsburgh Press, 2014.

Puri, Luv. "The Past and Future of Deobandi Islam." *CTC Sentinel*, Vol. 2, Issue 11, (November 2009): 19–22. https://ctc.usma.edu/.

Quigley, Carroll. *The Anglo-American Establishment: From Rhodes to Clivedon.* New York: Books in Focus, 1981.

Rex, Richard. *The Lollards.* Basingstoke: Palgrave, 2002.

BIBLIOGRAPHY

Richardson, Valerie. "Black Lives Matter cashes in with $100 million from liberal foundations." *The Washington Post*, August 16, 2016. http://www.washingtontimes.com/news/2016/aug/16/black-lives-matter-cashes-100-million-liberal-foun/.

Ridder-Symoens, Hilde. "Mobility." In *A History of the University in Europe*, edited by Walter Rüegg, 280–303. Cambridge: Cambridge University Press, 1992.

Ritchie, D.G. "Contributions to the History of Social Contract Theory." *Political Science Quarterly*, Vol. 6, No. 4 (December 1891): 656–76, http://www.jstor.org/stable/2139203.

Rockefeller Archive Center. "Other Organizations, Social Science Research Council Archives, 1924–1990." Accessed March 12, 2017. http://rockarch.org/collections/nonrockorgs/ssrc.php.

Roelofs, Joan. *Foundations and Public Policy: The Mask of Pluralism*. Albany: State University of New York Press, 2003.

Rosenfield, Patricia, and Rachel Wimpee. *The Ford Foundation Constant Themes, Historical Variations*. Rockefeller Archive Center, accessed March 9, 2019. https://rockarch.org/publications/ford/overview/FordFoundationHistory1936-2001.pdf.

Ross, Dorothy. "Changing Contours of the Social Science Disciplines." In *The Cambridge History of Science: The Modern Social Sciences*, edited by Theodore M. Porter, and Dorothy Ross, 205–38. Cambridge: Cambridge University Press, 2003.

Rothbard, Murray N. *Economic Thought before Adam Smith: An Austrian Perspective on the History of Economic Thought, Volume I*. Aldershot: Elgar, 1995.

Ryan, Yasmine. "How Tunisia's revolution began." *Al Jazeera*, January 26, 2011. http://www.aljazeera.com/indepth/features/2011/01/2011126121815985483.html.

Saak, Eric Leland. *Luther and the Reformation of the Later Middle Ages*. Cambridge: Cambridge University Press, 2017.

Salmon, J.H.M., ed. *The French Wars of Religion, How Important were Religious Factors?* Lexington: D.C. Heath and Company, 1967.

Samuel, Alan E. "Plutarch's Account of Solon's Reforms." *Greek, Roman, and Byzantine Studies*, Vol. 4, No. 4 (1963): 231–36. https://grbs.library.

duke.edu/index.

Saunders, Frances Stonor. *The Cultural Cold War: The CIA and the World of Arts and Letters*. New York: New Press, 2000.

Schaps, David M. *The Invention of Coinage and the Monetization of Ancient Greece*. Ann Arbor: University of Michigan Press, 2015.

Schonhardt-Bailey, Cheryl. *From the Corn Laws to Free Trade: Interests, Ideas, and Institutions in Historical Perspective*. Cambridge: MIT Press, 2006. https://www.jstor.org/stable/40750831.

Schoultz, Lars. *Human Rights and the United States Policy Toward Latin America*. Princeton: Princeton University Press, 1981.

Scott, Niall, and Jonathan Seglow. *Altruism*. Maidenhead: Open University Press, 2007.

Seaford, Richard. "Tragic Tyranny." In *Popular Tyranny: Sovereignty and Its Discontents in Ancient Greece,* edited by Kathyrn A. Morgan, 95–117. Austin: University of Texas Press, 2009.

Siedentop, Larry. *Inventing the Individual: The Origins of Western Liberalism*. Cambridge: Belknap Press of Harvard University Press, 2014.

Spufford, Peter. *Money and Its Use in Medieval Europe*. Cambridge: Cambridge University Press, 1988.

Stolberg, Sheryl Gay. "Shy U.S. Intellectual Created Playbook Used in a Revolution." *The New York Times*, February 16, 2011. https://www.nytimes.com/2011/02/17/world/middleeast/17sharp.html.

Staunton, Michael. *Thomas Becket and His Biographers*. Woodbridge: The Boydell Press, 2006.

Stephan, Walter, and Joe R. Feagin, *School Desegregation: Past, Present, and Future*. New York: Plenum Press, 1980.

Stockton, David. *The Classical Athenian Democracy*. New York: Oxford University Press, 1991.

Suarez, Francisco. "De legibus." III, 1.1, *Selection from Three Works of Francisco Suarez, S.J., Volume Two*. Oxford: Clarendon Press, 1944.

Taylor, Charles. *Sources of the Self: The Making of the Modern Identity*. Cambridge: Harvard University Press, 1989.

BIBLIOGRAPHY

Taylor, Quentin. "Descartes's Paradoxical Politics." *Humanitas*, Vol. 14, No. 2 (Fall 2001): 94–102. http://www.nhinet.org/taylor14-2.pdf.

Thomas, Emory M. *The Confederacy as a Revolutionary Experience*. Columbia: University of South Carolina Press, 1991.

Tierney, Brian. *Foundations of the Conciliar Theory: The Contribution of the Medieval Canonists from Gratian to the Great Schism*. Cambridge: Cambridge University Press, 1955.

Troeller, Gary. *The Birth of Saudi Arabia: Britain and the Rise of the House of Saud*. London: Routledge, 2013.

U.S. House of Representatives. Report of the Subcommittee on International Organizations and Movements of the Committee on Foreign Affairs. *Human Rights in the World Community: A Call for U.S. Leadership*. 93rd Congress, 2nd Session, 1974. Washington: GPO, 1974.

U.S. Senate. *In Response to Senate Resolution No. 220 (72nd Cong.) A Report on National Income, 1929–32, (Calendar Day, January 4), 1934*. 73rd Congress, 2nd Session, 1934, S. Doc. 124. Washington: GPO, 1934. https://fraser.stlouisfed.org/scribd/?title_id=971&filepath=/files/docs/publications/natincome_1934/19340104_nationalinc.pdf.

Vassiliev, Alexi. *The History of Saudi Arabia*. London: Saqi Books, 2000.

White House. "Freedom Agenda." Policies in Focus, President George W. Bush Archives. Accessed March 3, 2019. https://georgewbush-whitehouse.archives.gov/infocus/freedomagenda/.

Wierzbicka, Anna. *Imprisoned in English: The Hazards of English as a Default Language*. Oxford: Oxford University Press, 2014.

Wilford, Hugh. *The Mighty Wurlitzer: How the CIA Played America*. Cambridge: Harvard University Press, 2009.

Worth, Robert F. "How a Single Match Can Ignite a Revolution." *The New York Times*, January 21, 2001. https://www.nytimes.com/2011/01/23/weekinreview/23worth.html.

X, Malcolm. "Message to the Grass Roots." Speech, King Solomon Baptist Church, Detroit, MI, November 10, 1963. TeachingAmericanHistory.org. Accessed June 6, 2019. http://teachingamericanhistory.org/library/document/message-to-grassroots/.

CPSIA information can be obtained
at www.ICGtesting.com
Printed in the USA
LVHW082018301219
642043LV00004BA/492/P